THE BRIDGE PLAYER'S SUPPER BOOK

by Nicola Cox

GOOD FOOD FROM FARTHINGHOE
COUNTRY COOKING FROM FARTHINGHOE
NICOLA COX ON GAME COOKERY

THE BRIDGE PLAYER'S SUPPER BOOK

NICOLA COX

with a Foreword by

Elena Jeronimidis
Editor of *Bridge Plus*

VICTOR GOLLANCZ
in association with
PETER CRAWLEY

First published in Great Britain 1995
in association with Peter Crawley
by Victor Gollancz
An imprint of the Cassell Group
Wellington House, 125 Strand, London WC2R 0BB

A catalogue record for this book is available
from the British Library

ISBN 0 575 05945 1

Printed in Great Britain by
St Edmundsbury Press Ltd, Bury St Edmunds, Suffolk

Contents

Mousses

Omelettes

Cheese

Breads and Savouries

Salads and Vegetable Dishes

Main Dishes

Puddings

How to read the recipes
* Easy   ** Straightforward
*** More complicated
F Will freeze successfully
P Pre-preparation or planning required

Foreword

Bridge is a wonderful game. All you need to enjoy yourself is a table, four chairs, a pack of cards, pen and paper for scoring, and three other addicts. Although some *aficionados* might say that winning is sweeter if you play against people you *don't* like, most social players prefer to play in the company of friends—in which case supper will enhance the pleasure of bridge and congenial company alike.

Cooking for a bridge party, be it for four, eight, twelve or more players, has its own rules. Recipes must be easy to follow, or at least suitable for advance preparation, so as to leave the cook free to play without having to worry about repeated trips to the kitchen. If the party is to be a success, however, the food must not only meet the above requirements, but also be appealing to both eye and palate, which, you would think, rather restricts your choice of dishes.

Not so. This collection of specially selected recipes by Nicola Cox will prove that good food does not require slaving away at the stove when you should be concentrating on a delicate grand slam. I have tried several of these recipes, and both my family and bridge friends have voted them an unqualified success. As Editor of the magazine *Bridge Plus*, which publishes regular monthly recipes in our 'Dinner and Bridge' column, I know there is an avid demand for precisely the exciting sort of recipes given in *The Bridge Player's Supper Book*. Nicola Cox may not be a bridge player—yet—but as an experienced and imaginative cook she scores a top.

Elena Jeronimidis

Soups

F **   **Tomato and Tarragon Soup**

This is a lovely tasty tomato soup, just right for using up excess autumn tomatoes, and also good and reliable from the freezer. It's also a good soup to make for large numbers.

Ingredients
4–6 people

1½ lb (675g) fresh tomatoes or 1 × 1 lb 14
   oz (850g) approx tin of tomatoes
6 oz (175g) onion
1 stick celery
4 oz (100g) carrots
1½ oz (35g) butter
1 tbs olive oil
1 clove garlic
2 tbs tomato purée
½ bay leaf
1–2 tbs fresh or ½–¾ teasp dried
   tarragon
1¾ pts (1l) chicken stock or stock cube
   and water
1–2 teasp sugar to taste
1 small strip lemon rind
finely chopped parsley
salt and pepper

Finely slice the onion, celery and carrot (food processor with slicing blade). Melt the butter and oil in a saucepan, add the vegetables and cook gently until softened. Add the skinned and roughly chopped tomatoes (drained and chopped if you are using tinned ones, using the liquid as part of the stock quantity), chopped garlic, tomato purée, tarragon and bay leaf. Simmer for 20–30 minutes on gentle heat before adding the stock, sugar, lemon rind and seasoning. Simmer for 20 minutes longer, then purée, sieve and return to the rinsed-out pan. Check the seasoning, re-heat and serve sprinkled with finely chopped parsley.

*   Iced Cucumber Soup

Leave half the skin on the cucumber to make a delicate jade-coloured soup with a hint of mint. Cool to look at as well as on the tongue.

Ingredients
4–6 people

1 large cucumber
1 small finely chopped onion
1½ oz (35g) butter
½ oz (12g) flour
1½ pts (900ml) good white chicken or veal
    stock
a good sprig of mint

⅓ pt (200ml) cream
salt and pepper

Garnish
chopped chives
tiny dice of cucumber

Retain 2″ (5cm) cucumber to cube for garnish, and half peel and roughly dice the remainder. Melt the butter in a saucepan, add the onion and cucumber and gently 'sweat' for 4–5 minutes without browning. Sprinkle in the flour and stir, add the stock, mint and seasoning, and simmer for 20 minutes or so. Liquidise or purée very smooth and sieve. Chill. Blend in the cream, correct the seasoning and serve sprinkled with tiny dice of peeled cucumber and finely chopped chives.

F **   Smoked Haddock Chowder

A soup that's almost a meal; use more fish, potato and a handful of peas to make it a spoon-standing, one-course supper dish. I often make a thick version for the freezer and add more stock on thawing if I want it as a first-course soup.

Ingredients
4–6 people

1 lb (450g) smoked haddock fillet
2 pts (1.2l) chicken stock or water and
    stock-cubes
1 bay leaf
a good pinch mace
1 finely chopped onion
1 stick diced celery
2–3 peeled and diced potatoes
2 oz (50g) butter

1 teasp curry powder
1 oz (25g) flour
1 tbs oatmeal
½ pt (300ml) milk
¼ pt (150ml) cream (optional)
2 tbs parsley
2 tbs dry sherry
salt and pepper

Combine the skinned haddock in a saucepan with pepper, the bay leaf, mace and the chicken stock or water and cubes. Bring slowly to the boil and simmer for 5 minutes or until the fish will just flake. Flake the fish and set aside. In another large saucepan melt the butter and gently fry the onion and celery until golden, add the curry powder and flour and cook 2–3 minutes longer. Remove from the heat and wait for the sizzling to cease, then strain in the hot fish stock and bring to the boil, whisking hard and sprinkling on the oatmeal. Simmer for 10 minutes before adding the diced potato and flaked fish. Cook for 6–8 minutes or until the potatoes are tender. Add the milk and cream, correct the seasoning and heat through. Stir in the sherry and serve sprinkled with chopped parsley.

𝓕 *   Quick French Onion Soup

One should take ages to brown the onions gently, but it's surprising how you can speed it all up when you have to, and it's a good dish for a sudden late-night invasion. Cheddar cheese will do on top, but you will bless having some Gruyère in the freezer.

Ingredients
4–6 people

1 lb (450g) quite thickly sliced onions
3 oz (75g) dripping or butter and oil
2 teasp sugar
1 oz (25g) flour
2½ pts (1.5l) beef stock (or 1 beef cube, 2 pts (1.2l) water and a 10 fl oz (300ml) tin Campbell's Consommé)

4–6 slices stale French bread
4–6 tbs grated Gruyère or Cheddar cheese
1 egg yolk ⎫
3–4 tbs port or white wine ⎭ *optional*
salt and pepper

Heat the fat in a large frying pan or heavy casserole, add the sliced onions and sugar and fry fast for 10 minutes or so to a good brown; sprinkle on the flour and cook gently until lightly brown. Turn into a saucepan if necessary, add the stock (or cube, water and consommé) and bring to the boil, whisking. Season with a little salt and plenty of pepper and simmer for 5 minutes–1 hour depending on available time.

Place the bread in a soup tureen or individual bowls, ladle on the soup and scatter with cheese. Serve as it is, or brown under the grill, or pop in a hot oven (425°F/220°C/Gas 7) for about 10 minutes until golden brown and bubbling. If you are using the egg yolk and port or wine, whisk the yolk well and add the port. Slip a spoon under the cheesy crust and stir this mixture carefully into the soup just before serving.

F * ## Sweetcorn and Tuna Soup

Quickly made with a couple of tins, and a useful stand-by.

Ingredients
4–6 people

12 oz (350g) tin sweetcorn
3 oz (75g) tin tuna
2 oz (50g) butter
½ teasp curry powder
1½ oz (35g) flour
1 pt (600ml) chicken stock or water and
   stock-cubes
½ pt (300ml) milk

2 tbs sherry
finely chopped parsley
salt and pepper

Melt the butter and gently cook the curry powder and flour for 2–3 minutes. Off the stove add the chicken stock and milk, bring to the boil whisking hard and simmer 1–2 minutes. Stir in the sweetcorn and shredded tuna, season and heat through. Add the sherry and serve sprinkled with chopped parsley.

F * ## Curried Pea Soup

Pop it all in a pot, simmer and whizz; easy but good.

Ingredients
4–6 people

8 oz (225g) fresh or frozen peas
1 chopped onion
1 chopped carrot
1 chopped stick celery
1 large diced potato
1 teasp curry powder

½ teasp sugar
1½pt (900ml) chicken stock or water and
   stock-cubes
½ pt (300ml) milk
¼ pt (150ml) cream
fresh chopped dill or mint
croûtons
salt and pepper

Place the peas, onion, carrot, celery and potato in a saucepan, add the curry powder, sugar, salt, pepper and stock, cover and simmer for 15–20 minutes. Liquidise the soup until very smooth and add the milk and cream. Pass through a sieve and serve hot with a sprinkle of finely chopped mint or dill, and croûtons.

F **   Crème Louise

Iced summer soups are delicious and always popular. To get round the problem of too jellied a stock, resulting in a thick vegetable porridge, I often use a Chinese method of making stock. The chicken carcass, preferably raw, is chopped up into small bits to get the flavour from the marrow in the bones and boiled with flavouring ingredients for 1 hour only, during which time the liquid reduces by half. This will only set very lightly to jelly but will be full of flavour. This soup uses the felicitous combination of summer cucumber and tomato with cream and cream cheese to thicken it, yoghurt to freshen it and prawns to enhance it if you wish. Should you freeze it, it is good re-heated and served hot.

Ingredients
4–6 people

1 large cucumber
1 pt (600ml) approx white chicken stock
1 lb (450g) ripe tomatoes
3 oz (75g) cream cheese (optional)
½ pt (300 ml) plain yoghurt
¼ pt (150ml) whipping cream
2 oz (50g) peeled prawns (optional)
finely chopped chives
salt and pepper

Chinese Style White Chicken Stock
1 chicken carcass (preferably raw)
2 slices bacon (no fat or rind)
1 sliced small leek or onion
2–3 slices fresh root ginger
½ clove garlic
8 peppercorns
½ chicken stock cube
3 pts (1.7l) water
¼ teasp salt

Chinese Style White Chicken Stock. Chop the chicken carcass up, breaking the bones, using a chopper or strong kitchen scissors. Place in a saucepan with the remaining ingredients and bring to the boil. Skim well and boil for 1 hour, the pan half covered, so that the liquid reduces to about 1½ pts (900ml), of which you will need about 1 pt (600ml), skimming from time to time. Strain through muslin or a fine sieve and remove any fat after standing a few minutes or when cold.

Peel and slice the cucumber and cook until tender in ½ pt (300ml) of the chicken stock. Process until smooth, then strain into a bowl; I use a liquidiser in preference to a food processor because it produces a more velvety result. Process the roughly chopped tomatoes with the remaining ½ pt (300ml) of stock and sieve into the bowl. Mix the cream cheese, if used, yoghurt and cream until smooth, or process briefly. Strain into the bowl and whisk all together. Check seasoning and chill well. Serve in chilled bowls, scattered with prawns, if used, and chopped chives.

F **   # Potato and Watercress Soup

This potato and watercress soup, made with good chicken stock and served with or without the cream and egg yolk liaison, is simple but excellent.

Ingredients
4–6 people

1½ lb (675g) peeled potatoes
1 good bunch watercress
1½ pts (900ml) chicken stock
good squeeze lemon juice
3 fl oz (75ml) cream (optional)
1 egg yolk (optional)
fresh chopped chervil (optional)
fried croûtons (optional)
salt and pepper

Cut the potatoes into even-sized pieces and boil, just covered in lightly salted water, until tender. While they cook, chop up and simmer the watercress stalks in the chicken stock for about 20 minutes; then strain, pressing the stalks well. Drain the potatoes, retaining some of the water, and sieve or pass through a potato masher back into the saucepan. Dilute with the strained, watercress-flavoured chicken stock. When nearly ready to serve, chop the watercress leaves and stir in with a good squeeze of lemon juice and season.

For a richer, smoother soup, whisk the egg yolk with the cream and gradually whisk in some of the hot soup. Return to the pan. Heat the soup gently but *do not boil* or the egg may curdle.

If you wish, serve sprinkled with a little finely chopped chervil and hand tiny hot croûtons of bread, fried in butter and olive oil. I love the delicacy of this soup, but you can, if you like, make it more positive with two bunches of watercress.

F *   # Etta's Tomato Soup

I first learned to cook at about the age of eight with my grandmother's cook Etta. She made cakes and biscuits with me and I used to watch her at work in the kitchen as I ate my supper. Things learned at that age stay so clearly in the mind, and I still see the perfectly formed, tiny dice of tomato appearing from under her huge steel knife at incredible speed. This soup is really only a white sauce base, thinned with chicken stock and served with diced tomato and chopped parsley. It's simple and good, and useful when you have only a few, fine-flavoured tomatoes.

Ingredients
4–6 people

2 oz (50g) butter	3 firm tasty tomatoes
1½ oz (35g) flour	1–2 tbs finely chopped parsley or chives
½ pt (300ml) milk	salt and pepper
1¾ pts (1l) good white chicken stock	

Melt the butter in a saucepan and add the flour. Cook, stirring, over moderate heat for 2–3 minutes, then draw off the stove and wait for the sizzling to cease. Add the milk and return to the heat. Bring to the boil, whisking hard, and simmer for 1–2 minutes before seasoning with salt and pepper. Now gradually thin this white sauce with the chicken stock to cream soup consistency (¼ or ½ a chicken stock cube can be added if the stock is lacking in flavour).

Meanwhile skin the tomatoes. Cut them in half round their middles, squeeze out and discard the pips and cut the tomato flesh into even, small dice. Add to the soup with the fairly finely chopped parsley or chives and correct the seasoning only when ready to serve, for the tomato should keep its freshness and shape. The creamy coloured soup is very pretty with its dice of tomato and green flecks of parsley.

F * ## Soupe de Courge

Those naughty courgettes which grow from finger-length to hand-sized while one's back is turned will still make a very nice soup. I like to serve it with fried croûtons and grated Gruyère, as the French serve pumpkin soup.

Ingredients
4–6 people

	To Finish (optional)
1½ lb (675g) courgettes	croûtons
1 onion	grated Gruyère cheese
1 oz (25g) butter	
1 pt (600ml) good stock	
½ pt (300ml) milk	
a little cream (optional)	
salt and pepper	

Soften the onion gently in butter, add the skinned, de-seeded and sliced courgettes, the stock and seasoning and simmer gently for 20–30 minutes until absolutely tender. Purée and sieve back into the pan, add the milk and some cream if you like, and correct the seasoning. Heat the croûtons and hand with a bowl of grated cheese.

* Creamed Mushroom Consommé

When time is at a premium this mixture of tinned consommé, cream and wafers of fresh baby mushrooms is well worth knowing.

Ingredients
4–6 people

2 tins Campbell's condensed beef
   consommé
2 teasp dried tarragon
2 oz (50g) button mushrooms
½ pt (300ml) whipping cream
½–1 teasp potato flour

squeeze of lemon juice
finely chopped chervil or parsley
salt and pepper

Heat the consommé with the tarragon and infuse for 10–15 minutes. Strain, add the very finely sliced mushrooms and simmer for 3–4 minutes. Mix the potato flour with a little cream, add and boil to thicken. Pour in the rest of the cream and heat through. Correct the seasoning, add a squeeze of lemon juice and serve scattered with chopped chervil or parsley.

ℱ * Publisher's Leek Soup

We are rather inclined to make smooth soup with our modern machinery. This simple soup, for which I have to thank my publisher Peter Crawley, has generous bits of leek in it, and makes a really comforting soup. It provides a cosy supper dish if you cube and dry some stale brown bread, preferably home-made, in the oven. Put in the bottom of the soup bowl with a handful of grated cheese, and ladle over the soup.

Ingredients
4–6 people

¾–1 lb (350–450g) white and tender
   green leeks
1½ oz (35g) butter
1½ oz (35g) flour
2 pts (1.2l) good stock
¼ pt (150ml) milk
½ chicken stock cube

1 bay leaf
good pinch mace
salt and pepper

To Serve
croûtons
a little grated cheese (optional)
chopped parsley (optional)

Wash the leeks well and cut them in half lengthways so that you can rinse the mud from between the leaves. Cut them into slices between ½"–1" (1–2cm) thick, thinner for elegant soup or thicker for a more rustic character. Melt the butter in a heavy pan or casserole (earthenware gives a good flavour) and fry gently, covered, without browning to sweat the leeks for about 20–30 minutes. Remove the pan from the heat and stir in the flour. Add the stock and milk and return to the stove. Add a pinch of mace, the bay leaf and stock cube and bring to the boil whilst stirring. Simmer for 20 minutes before serving. Serve with croûtons, a little grated cheese or some chopped parsley if you wish.

F * ## Rich Mushroom Soup

This soup has a real home-made taste and a rich flavour of mushrooms. It also freezes extremely well.

Ingredients
4–6 people

½ lb (225g) fresh mushrooms
1 oz (25g) butter
1½ pts (900ml) good stock
1 tbs potato flour
½ pt (300ml) milk
salt and pepper

To Finish
a few drops of lemon juice
1 oz (25g) butter
2–4 tbs cream
some finely chopped chervil or parsley

Melt the butter in a saucepan, add the finely sliced mushrooms and cook very gently with the lid on for 5–10 minutes. Add the stock, season and simmer for ½ hour or so. Mix the potato flour and milk until smooth and add to the soup. Simmer for 10 minutes more and then liquidise (you get a more velvety smooth soup using a liquidiser for this recipe rather than a food processor).

Return to the pan and heat up, add lemon juice to taste and the cream. Check the seasoning and finish with the butter (whisked in off the stove in small flakes) and serve with chopped chervil or parsley stirred in.

F *   # Chicken or Turkey Soup

There are many styles of chicken soup, but I find this one is simple and quick and really tastes of chicken. It is the generous quantity of butter that gives it its smooth texture and lovely flavour.

Ingredients
4–6 people

2½ oz (60g) butter
1½ oz (35g) plain flour
1½ pts (900ml) chicken or turkey stock
½ pt (300ml) milk

½ chicken stock cube (optional)
any scraps of cooked chicken or turkey, cubed
chopped parsley
salt and pepper

Melt the butter in a saucepan, add the flour and cook over moderate heat, stirring, for 2–3 minutes. Draw the pan off the stove, wait for the sizzling to cease and add the stock, stock cube (if used) and milk. Bring to the boil, whisking with a wire whisk (use a wooden spoon round the edge of the pan so that no flour sticks there) and simmer for 2–3 minutes. Add any cubed cooked chicken or turkey and the chopped parsley, correct the seasoning, re-heat and serve.

*   # Hot-Sour Soup

This appetising, piquant soup has a rather Chinese character. Whenever you have some good stock, it can be quickly put together with whatever of the ingredients you happen to have. A packet of dried cèpe or Chinese mushrooms pre-soaked in warm water heightens the flavour. For crunchy contrasting textures serve the moment it is made.

Ingredients
4–6 people

2 pts (1.2l) good chicken, turkey or game stock
½ small clove garlic
½ onion or 2 spring onions
½ chicken stock cube (optional)
2 oz (50g) finely sliced cooked chicken (optional)
2 oz (50g) sliced button mushrooms
  or 2 dried Chinese mushrooms
  or a few bits of dried cèpe soaked in warm water for ½ hour

a little grated root ginger
3 oz (75g) frozen green peas
1 teasp sugar
2 tbs soy sauce
2 tbs vinegar
½ teasp chilli sauce
2–3 teasp cornflour
2 oz (50g) frozen prawns
finely chopped chives, parsley or coriander (optional)
a few drops sesame oil (optional)
salt and pepper only if necessary

Cut the garlic into tiny slivers and the onion into wafer thin slices and add to the stock with the stock cube, chicken, sliced mushrooms, grated ginger and peas. Add the sugar, soy, vinegar and chilli sauce and bring to the boil. Stir in the cornflour, slaked in a little cold water. Boil for just another minute or two until thickened and clear, then add the prawns, chopped herbs and a few drops of sesame oil (if used). Test for seasoning and serve at once.

F ** Creamy Onion Soup

It's a help to have recipes using ingredients which are usually around. This creamy white soup, which is nicest with a generous hint of nutmeg or mace, can be finished with cream, or not, as you please.

Ingredients
4–6 people

1 lb (450g) roughly chopped onions
1½ pts (900ml) stock
1½ oz (35g) butter
1½ oz (35g) flour
½ pt (300ml) milk
¼ pt (150ml) cream (optional)
½–1 oz (12–25g) butter to finish
freshly grated nutmeg or pinch mace
salt and pepper

Simmer the onions in the stock with the seasoning for 30–40 minutes or until tender; drain and reserve the liquid. Melt the butter, add the flour and cook over moderate heat, stirring, for 2–3 minutes; then draw the pan off the stove, and when the sizzling ceases add the milk. Bring to the boil, whisking hard, and simmer for 2–3 minutes.

Purée the onions and add. Thin with the reserved onion stock, correct the seasoning and add a good grate of nutmeg or pinch of mace. Finish with the cream, if used, and add flakes of butter stirred in off the stove.

Pâtés

ℱ *   Smoked Mackerel Pâté

A smooth light pâté, quick to whip up and appreciated at any time of the year.

Ingredients
4–6 people

2 smoked mackerel fillets, together
    weighing about 12 oz (350g)
4 oz (100g) butter
¼ pt (150ml) cream
1 lemon
salt, pepper and mace

Gently melt the butter. Skin the mackerel, place the flesh in a food processor or liquidiser and process, adding the butter, lemon juice and seasoning. Turn into a bowl and when cold fold in the softly whipped cream and any additional lemon juice to taste. Pack into containers. Serve at room temperature for full flavour and creaminess.

ℱ **   Pâté de Foie de Volaille

A chicken liver pâté which is not harsh or too strong in flavour. It freezes well, being rich and creamy, but do thaw it really well and serve at room temperature for the maximum creaminess and full flavour. A little goes a long way, and it's well worth having a few small pots handy.

Ingredients
6 people

½ lb (225g) chicken livers
1 small onion, finely chopped
1 clove garlic
1 tbs fresh herbs (parsley, thyme, chervil
    tarragon, savory or what you will)

5 oz (125g) butter
¼ pt (150ml) cream
1 tbs sherry
salt, pepper and ground allspice

Pick over the livers, carefully removing any threads and green-tinged flesh. Melt 2 oz (50g) butter and gently fry the onion for 4–5 minutes. Add the chicken livers and sauté over high heat until lightly browned, stir in the chopped garlic and herbs and season well. Cover and cook gently for 4–5 minutes. Cool a little, then scrape all into a food processor or liquidiser and process; when smooth, add the remaining butter, sherry and cream and give one final quick whizz. Pour into pots and cool. Serve at room temperature.

ℱ *   Smoked Salmon Pâté

Quick, easy and light as air, this delicate pâté does nothing to detract from the flavour of the salmon.

Ingredients
4 people

4 oz (100g) smoked salmon bits
3 oz (75g) butter

2½ fl oz (60ml) cream
lemon juice
salt, pepper and paprika

Melt the butter. Place the roughly chopped smoked salmon in a food processor or liquidiser, turn on and add the butter in a thin stream. Process until very smooth, season and cool. Whip the cream and fold into the cold salmon mixture with lemon juice to taste. Check the seasoning and turn into a pot. Serve at room temperature with hot toast, brioche toast or fresh bread.

*   Sardine Pâté

A tasty sardine spread which will do well in an emergency.

Ingredients
4–6 people

2 tins sardines
3 oz (75g) butter
1–2 tbs green peppercorns

⅛ teasp mace
1 lemon
salt

Cream the butter well, beat in the drained sardines and season with salt, a good sprinkle of mace, a little grated lemon rind and the green peppercorns. Beat well and add a good squeeze of lemon juice (this can all be done very quickly in the food processor with metal blade). Pack into a pot or mound on to a dish and chill. Serve with toast, bread, buns or biscuits. Also very nice for open sandwiches, spread thickly on crustless brown bread and garnished with slices of hard-boiled egg, olives and strips of dill cucumber.

ℱ * **Rillettes**

A speciality from the Touraine region of France which is easy and inexpensive to make. It is unusual, but seems to be enjoyed by everyone I've tried it on. It freezes very well or will keep in the fridge for some time.

Ingredients
6–8 people

1 lb (450g) meaty belly of pork
½ lb (225g) pork fat (back fat or flair)
1 oz (25g) lard or pork dripping
½ clove garlic
2 tbs water
sprig of thyme
¼ teasp quatre épices or pinch of cloves,
    nutmeg, cinnamon and ginger
salt and pepper

Cut the meat and fat into ½" × 1½" (1cm × 4cm) strips. Melt the lard in a heavy pan, add the meat, pork fat, the water, the crushed clove of garlic and the thyme and seasoning. Cover and cook in a slow oven (300°F/150°C/Gas 2) for about 4 hours (or it can be cooked *very* gently on the top of the stove). When very soft, tender and well cooked, pour the mixture into a sieve over a bowl to separate the fat. Then pound the meat in a mortar or process briefly in a food processor with a plastic blade to form a thready pâté. Check the seasoning and pack into terrines. Covered with the strained fat (but *no* meaty juices) to a depth of ½" (1.5cm), your rillettes should keep for 6 months to one year in a cool dry larder, though I feel happier freezing them. Serve at room temperature with fresh bread.

Smoked Cod's Roe Special

Ingredients
4–6 people

8 oz (225g) smoked cod's roe
3–4 oz (75–100g) soft butter
½ clove garlic (optional)
juice of ½–1 lemon (approx)
shake of tabasco sauce to taste
1 tbs chopped parsley
2–4 tbs cream (optional)
pepper
salt only if necessary

If the cod's roe is rather hard and dry, soak it in hot water for a few minutes to make it easier to skin. Smoked cod's roe can vary from the very dry and salty to quite soft and delicate, so use your discretion, and don't hesitate to add more butter or cream if it needs it. Peel the smoked roe. Cream the butter until really soft, or process in a food processor, then add the roe and crushed garlic, if used, and beat together until light. Add lemon juice to taste and season with tabasco and pepper. Add the parsley and, depending on how strongly flavoured it is, a little cream to soften the flavour. Pack into pots and serve with hot melba toast or bread as a starter or on biscuits or packed into sticks of celery to go with drinks.

*   Guacamole

This Mexican avocado pâté, hot or mild as you please, makes a good first course or cocktail party dip with crunchy vegetables or crisp toast.

Ingredients
4–6 people

2 ripe avocado pears
2 spring onions
1 clove garlic
2 limes or 1 lemon
few drops Tabasco or Mexican green
    pepper sauce to taste
4–6 tbs olive oil
3–4 peeled, seeded and finely diced
    tomatoes
2 tbs finely diced celery
2 tbs finely diced green pepper
1 tbs finely chopped parsley
salt

Peel the avocados and crush the flesh or process in the food processor. Add the chopped onion and garlic crushed with salt. Season with Tabasco. Beat well and drip in the oil and lime or lemon juice (made in a food processor it becomes a wonderful smooth mixture). Stir in by hand the chopped tomato, celery, pepper and parsley. Turn into a bowl and press cling film or wet greaseproof paper on to the mixture to delay discolouring. Do not make this too far ahead. Serve with fresh bread or crisp toast, or with lengths of raw vegetables, celery, carrot or cauliflower.

F *   Goose or Duck Pâté

Any little scraps of meat you can winkle off the carcass can be made into a little pot of pâté. Use some goosefat, if you have it, as well as butter, for it gives a lovely texture and flavour to the pâté.

Ingredients
6–8 people

½ lb (225g) cooked scraps of goose or
  duck meat and fat without skin, bone
  or sinew
2–3 oz (50–75g) soft butter, or mixed
  goosefat and butter
2 tbs Madeira or sherry
salt, pepper and mace

Process, mince or pound the meat until smooth, then work in the butter, fat, seasoning and Madeira or sherry. Pack into pots. Serve at room temperature with hot toast and lemon wedges.

F *   Smoked Haddock Pâté

One of the simplest yet nicest of smoked haddock pâtés, which freezes well and is also popular at parties.

Ingredients
4–6 people

8 oz (225g) smoked haddock fillet
4 tbs milk (approx)
4 oz (100g) soft butter
½ bay leaf
1″ (3cm) thick slice crustless white or
  brown bread made into breadcrumbs
½ teasp anchovy essence
½ lemon
salt, pepper, paprika and ground mace

Skin the haddock fillet and put in a saucepan with the milk, half the butter, the bay leaf, a little sprinkle of mace and salt and rather more pepper and paprika. Cook over gentle heat until the fish will just flake, but do not over-cook.

Pour the milk from the fish over the breadcrumbs in a food processor or liquidiser, add the flaked fish, anchovy essence and lemon juice. Process, and add the remaining soft butter. Adjust seasoning and pack into pots, where it will firm up a bit on cooling.

Serve cold with hot toast and lemon quarters.

Mousses

** Egg Mousse

This is a delicious egg mousse, smooth and creamy with a thick layer of chopped chives topped with a deep brown translucent layer of jelly. Make well ahead, as the consommé takes time to set, and do make sure you get one which will set to jelly, so check the instructions on the can. When you have not got masses of chives, use the diced celery and pepper.

Ingredients
4–6 people

4 hard-boiled eggs
1 pt (600ml) Campbell's beef consommé
⅓ pt (200ml) cream
1 teasp anchovy essence
1 teasp Worcester sauce
1 slice onion
1 teasp tarragon vinegar

2 teasp gelatine
½ lemon
lots of chives *or* 1 stick celery and
   1 slice green pepper
salt and pepper

Sprinkle the gelatine on to 2 tablespoonfuls of consommé in a little bowl, leave to soak for a few moments and stand in a pan of hot water to melt. Stir into the rest of the consommé with the tarragon vinegar and a good squeeze of lemon juice, and set half of it aside. Place the remainder, the chopped-up eggs, anchovy essence, Worcester sauce, slice of onion and seasoning in the liquidiser and process until absolutely smooth. In a food processor, process the egg until quite smooth before adding the remaining ingredients. Pour through a sieve into a large bowl and chill, stirring from time to time until it begins to thicken. Whip the cream until it is just holding its shape and fold in. Pour into a 2-pint or 1-litre soufflé dish or glass bowl and leave to set in the fridge.

Cover very thickly with chopped chives or the celery and green pepper cut into very tiny dice, then spoon over a little of the reserved consommé (warm it gently if it has already set). Leave this to set before pouring over the rest of the reserved consommé (if you don't the chives will float to the top and spoil it). This will keep in the fridge for 1–2 days and is nice served with little cress sandwiches or melba toast.

ℱ *   # Ham Mousse

This smooth and delicate pale pink mousse is useful for a cold lunch or supper.

Ingredients
4–6 people

½ lb (225g) lean ham diced
1 teasp tomato purée
8 fl oz (225ml) good stock
2 tbs dry white wine

¼ oz (6g) gelatine (1½ level teasp)
1–1½ tbs dry sherry
¼ pt (150ml) cream
salt, pepper, and nutmeg

Sprinkle the gelatine on to the white wine in a small cup. Leave to soak for a minute or two, then stand in a saucepan of hot water to melt. Either process the ham in a food processor until smooth, then pour on the stock, the melted gelatine and tomato purée; or place the ham, stock, melted gelatine and tomato purée in a liquidiser and process until smooth. Turn into a bowl, season well and add the sherry. Chill in the fridge, stirring from time to time until almost set, or stand in a bowl of ice and water and stir until nearly set. Beat the cream until just holding its shape and fold carefully into the mousse. Turn into a dish and chill for several hours or overnight before serving.

ℱ *   # Smoked Trout Mousse

Simple and quick to make, this delicious mousse is a firm favourite.

Ingredients
4–6 people

8 oz (225g) smoked trout
6 oz (175g) cream cheese (Eden Vale
    Somerset soft cream cheese for choice)
¼ pt (150ml) plain yoghurt
2 teasp gelatine
2 tbs white wine

½ teasp horseradish sauce
a squeeze of lemon juice
¼ pt (150ml) cream
¼ cucumber
salt, pepper and nutmeg

Sprinkle the gelatine on to the white wine in a cup, soak for several minutes, then stand in a saucepan of hot water to dissolve. Skin and bone the smoked trout and flake into a food processor or liquidiser. Process until finely chopped, then add the cream cheese and yoghurt. Season with salt, pepper and nutmeg and add the horseradish, the melted gelatine and lemon juice to taste. Turn into a bowl. Fold in the cream, whipped until just holding its shape. Put in a 1 pt (600ml) soufflé dish and chill. Decorate with sliced cucumber and serve with thin brown bread and butter.

F **   Smoked Haddock Mousse

Process the eggs to an absolutely smooth texture so that you can freeze this mousse if you wish (pieces of hard-boiled eggs go rubbery and uneatable in the freezer). Its delicate flavour and fine texture make it a good first course or light lunch dish. Try making it in a ring mould, filling the centre with a sliced tomato and Florence fennel salad, dressed with a little basil and a good oil and lemon juice dressing.

Ingredients
4–6 people

¾ lb (350g) smoked haddock
¼ pt (150ml) milk
2 eggs
2 tbs white wine
2 teasp gelatine
¼ pt (150ml) mayonnaise
¼ pt (150ml) whipping cream
a squeeze of lemon juice
pepper and mace

To Decorate
sliced cucumber, hard-boiled egg, or a
   few prawns and parsley

Hard boil the eggs. Simmer the skinned haddock in the milk until cooked. Drain, remove bones, flake and make the cooking milk up to ¼ pt (150ml), no more.

Sprinkle the gelatine gradually on to the white wine in a small bowl, leave to soak for several minutes, then stand the bowl in a pan of hot water to melt. Process the hard-boiled eggs in a food processor until very smooth, add the fish and process until that is also very smooth (with a liquidiser, process fish, eggs and liquid together). Add the measured cooking milk, gelatine and seasoning, leave to cool, then add the mayonnaise. When just beginning to set, fold in the cream, whipped until it is just holding its shape; correct seasoning and add a squeeze of lemon juice. Turn into a 1 pt (600ml) soufflé dish and chill. Serve decorated with sliced cucumber, hard-boiled egg or a few prawns and parsley.

Omelettes

** **Cold Prawn Omelette**

I like to serve this barely lukewarm for a summer supper, making individual omelettes or two larger ones that can be divided. I have included the method for making prawn butter, but if you have some in the freezer (it freezes well), this dish can be very quickly and easily made with a packet of frozen prawns.

Ingredients
2–3 people (or for 4–6 as a starter)

6 eggs
½ oz (12g) butter
salt and pepper

Prawn filling
6 oz (175g) prawns in their shells
2 oz (50g) butter
½–1 teasp flour
4–6 tbs cream
a pinch mace
salt and pepper

Prawn filling. Shell the prawns and add the shells to the melted butter in a frying pan. Toss over high heat for a few minutes, then turn into a food processor or liquidiser and process until well chopped. Scrape the mixture into a square of muslin and squeeze out all the prawn butter. Melt 1 oz (25g) or so of prawn butter in a pan and add the prawns; toss over moderate heat for 10–15 seconds and season with pepper and mace. Sprinkle on a little flour and cook gently for several moments before adding the cream and simmering to make a thick creamy sauce. Correct the seasoning.

Break 2–3 eggs into a bowl, season and whisk with a fork. Heat an omelette pan and, when very hot, add a scrap of butter; once melted, pour in the egg and make an omelette, spooning on some of the filling when nearly done. Fold and turn out. Make the remaining omelettes. Leave to cool and serve with fresh rolls, butter and a salad.

** Frittata alla Genovese

Egg and spinach fritters. Into the pan and on to the plate, or served cold.

Ingredients
4–6 people

3–4 eggs
½ eggshell cold water
4–6 oz (100–175g) spinach, cooked,
   squeezed and chopped

chopped parsley, lemon thyme or
   marjoram
1 tbs freshly grated Parmesan
salt, pepper and nutmeg
a little oil for frying

Beat the eggs with the cold water and add the chopped spinach, herbs and seasoning. Heat a little oil in a frying pan and place large spoonfuls of the mixture (which should be stiff enough to hold its shape) in the pan to make 3"–4" (8cm–10cm) pancakes. Cook to a light brown on both sides. Eat at once, perhaps slipped inside a fresh buttered bap or served with Italian Tomato Sauce, or leave to cool and serve sprinkled with a herby vinaigrette dressing at a summer meal or picnic.

* Asparagus Omelette

Make this either with the very first few tender spears or when there is only a little bit of asparagus, especially those thin shoots sold as 'sprue'. It can be served hot or cold, and is wonderful cold on a hot spring or summer's day.

Ingredients
2–3 people as a main course
4–6 people as a starter

6–8 oz (175–225g) thinnish asparagus or
   3–4 oz (75–100g) cooked asparagus
   tips
6–8 eggs

1½ oz (35g) butter
½–1 teasp flour
4–6 tbs whipping cream or top of the
   milk
salt and pepper

Cook the asparagus in lightly salted boiling water, drain and refresh under the cold tap to set the colour. Cut the tender tops into 2–3 pieces and set aside. Discard tough stalks or keep for soup.

Heat 1 oz (25g) of the butter in a small pan, toss the cut asparagus in the hot butter, then sprinkle over a little flour. Cook for a moment or two before adding the cream or top of milk, off the stove. Boil up, stirring gently, and season.

Make your omelettes (*see page 30*), using 2–4 eggs at a time, depending on the size of your pan; when nearly cooked, spoon some filling across the middle of each. Fold over and turn out. Serve at once or leave to cool and serve cold with a salad.

Cheese

** Cheese Aigrettes

Only recently did I discover that these could be deep-fried and would keep warm for a couple of hours. So into the repertoire went the recipe.

Ingredients
4–6 people

2 oz (50g) butter
¼ pt (150ml) water
4 oz (100g) 'strong' flour
4 eggs (not larger than No. 3)
4–6 oz (100–175g) strong cheese (half
    Parmesan, half Gruyère or Cheddar)

1 teasp Dijon mustard
paprika
½ teasp salt
pepper

deep fat for frying

Place the chopped-up butter, water and salt in a saucepan and heat. Once the butter has melted bring to the boil. Draw off the heat, tip in all the sifted flour at once and stir until a ball of dough forms and comes away from the side of the pan. Cook over moderate heat for 1–2 minutes, stirring, until a skin forms on the bottom of the pan. Remove from the heat and cool for 5–10 minutes. Beat in the eggs one at a time, beating hard after each addition; the mixture must remain firm enough to sit up on the spoon, so add the last egg gradually if you feel the mixture is getting too soft—it should be smooth and shiny. Or turn into a food processor, add all the eggs and process for 30–45 seconds until satiny smooth. Beat in the grated cheese, mustard and pepper.

Heat the deep fat to 375°F/190°C or until just hazing, then add very small teaspoonfuls of the mixture, not too many at a time, and cook until puffed up and crisp and a good brown colour. Drain on kitchen paper, sprinkle with salt and paprika, spread out on a dish and keep hot until ready to serve. Serve piled up and watch them disappear like snow off a dyke. This makes plenty (the batches will take quite a long time to fry) but they always all disappear!

* Potted Cheese with Herbs

I find it so useful to be able to turn a tired or deep-frozen bit of cheddar into something delectable for the cheese board. Cheddar Cheese with Walnuts is a firm winter favourite, but in summer I prefer to pot up my Cheddar with herbs and white wine. Personally I like to serve this soon after it is made, soft and creamy, but of course it will keep in the fridge for a week or so if you wish. In winter, or if you have no fresh herbs, use chopped celery leaves from the top of the sticks or Florence fennel fronds; celery sticks or Florence fennel wedges are good served with this anyway. Chopped watercress can be used too, especially if it's quite strong and peppery, so even without fresh herbs or a garden you can still make this recipe.

Ingredients
Makes about 1¼ lb (550g)

12 oz (350g) mature Cheddar, Leicester or Gloucester cheese
4 oz (100g) butter
6 tbs dry white wine

4–5 tbs chopped fresh herbs (chives, summer savory, lemon thyme, fennel, celery leaf or rocket)
½ teasp paprika

Cream the butter really well until it is very soft and creamy so that it can absorb the wine. Grate the cheese and cream it in with the butter, ideally in a food processor. Warm the wine a little (it combines with the butter and cheese more easily if slightly warm) and gradually beat it in with the herbs and paprika to taste. Mound on to a cheese board or pack into a pot. I sometimes press it into a muslin-lined mould (you could use a *petit coeur à la crème* mould for this) to turn out like a little sand-castle or heart. You can coat with chopped herbs, coarsely crushed peppercorns, halved black olives or paprika, if you wish.

*   Cheddar Cheese with Walnuts

We make this with Cheddar cheese from the freezer, and even when I'm offering a good cheese board everyone seems to go for it.

Ingredients
Makes about 1¼ lb (550g)

12 oz (350g) mature Cheddar cheese
4 oz (100g) butter
6 tbs stout, beer or lager

mustard and Worcester sauce (optional)
pepper
4 oz (100g) walnut halves

Grate the cheese. Cream the butter until soft, beat in the grated cheese and gradually work in stout or beer until creamy (very quick with the food processor). Season with pepper and add mustard and Worcester sauce if the cheese is poor in flavour.

Line a round pot with muslin, line the base with walnut halves, pack in half the cheese, put another layer of walnuts in the middle, then the remaining cheese. Turn out before serving. Or mound the cheese into a good shape and press walnuts all over the surface. Chill. Can be used almost at once, but the walnuts become moist and succulent if it's made 24 hours ahead. Will keep for a week or more.

Breads and Savouries

ℱ ** Brioche Loaf

Easy to make, delicious, impressive, and good with rich pâtés.

Ingredients *1 loaf*

8 oz (225g) 'strong' white flour
½ oz (12g) fresh yeast
4 fl oz (100ml) tepid milk
1 tbs white sugar

4 oz (100g) butter
2 eggs
½ teasp salt

Cream the sugar and yeast until runny and stir in the milk. Sieve the flour and salt into a bowl or food processor. Rub in the butter until it is of breadcrumb consistency, then add the yeast mixture and the eggs to make a very soft dough. Beat with your hand or a wooden spoon for 10 minutes (or 1 minute in the food processor).

Scrape the mixture from the sides of the bowl, cover with a plastic bag or damp cloth and leave to rise for about 1 hour until double in size. Knead for a few moments or process for 10 seconds and turn into an oiled 1 lb (450g) loaf tin or brioche mould. Cover with the plastic bag and leave to double in bulk and fill the mould, again for about 1 hour. Transfer carefully to a moderately hot oven (375°F/190°C/Gas 5) and bake for 35–40 minutes. Cover the top if it starts getting too brown. Turn out on to a wire rack and cool. If time is short turn the dough into the tin after kneading, allow to rise only once, and cook.

* Sesame Fingers

Crisp bread fingers crowded with sesame seeds make a nice crunchy accompaniment for any smooth first course where contrast is needed.

Ingredients *16 fingers*

4 slices white or brown bread
2–3 oz (50–75g) butter

sesame seeds
salt

Take the crusts off the bread and cut into fingers. Dip both sides briefly in the melted butter, place on a rack, sprinkle heavily with sesame seeds and season. Cook in a slow oven (300°F/150°C/Gas 2) until crisp right through. Serve hot or cold to accompany soups, mousses or anything where a little crunch is needed to complete the effect.

Salads and Vegetable Dishes

* Leeks au Gratin

Leeks are a wonderful winter vegetable, standing for long months in the garden or readily available in the shops. They need careful cleaning as there is nothing worse than crunching on grit as you eat them; if you slit them down one side, cutting part way through, you can run them under the tap, washing earth and grit out from between each half. Sliced and braised gently in a little butter until meltingly tender, they can be served just like that, or turned into a fashionable purée with a little cream or *beurre noisette*. You can also bind them with a little potato flour and milk and serve them almost as a leek porridge. My mother uses a slab of bread as a sponge, or the up-side-down saucer technique to drain off unwanted liquid which tends to gather under leeks; the leeks are laid over the saucer in a dish, and the moisture gathers in the bottom. Whole or cut up and carefully cooked and drained, leeks are nice in a white sauce; topped with cheese and breadcrumbs and browned, they become one of those superb simple dishes so much enjoyed by gourmets.

Ingredients
4–6 people

1½–2 lb (675–900g) prepared leeks,
  white and tender green
4 oz (100g) grated Cheddar or Gruyère
  cheese
3–4 tbs breadcrumbs
a few flakes butter
salt and pepper

Sauce
1½ oz (35g) butter
1 oz (25g) plain flour
15 fl oz (450g) milk
salt, pepper and nutmeg

Carefully wash the leeks and cook in boiling salted water for about 10–20 minutes until just tender. Drain well and lay them neatly in a buttered gratin dish, season with salt and pepper and pour over the sauce. Sprinkle with cheese and breadcrumbs, top with a few flakes of butter and brown under the grill.

Sauce. Melt the butter in a saucepan, add the flour and cook, stirring, over moderate heat for 2–3 minutes; then draw the pan off the heat, wait for the sizzling to cease and add the milk. Bring to the boil, whisking well, season and simmer very gently until of good coating consistency.

** Mushrooms or Courgettes à la Grecque

Mushrooms or baby courgettes in a syrupy, herby juice. Serve with fresh rolls or hot garlic bread or as part of a mixed Hors d'Oeuvre.

Ingredients
4–6 people

1 lb (450g) firm button mushrooms or
   little courgettes cut into 1″ (2–3cm)
   fingers
½ pt (300ml) water
6 tbs olive oil
6 tbs lemon juice
2 tbs finely chopped onion

a bundle of parsley, celery and fennel (or
   use fennel seeds) and thyme
10 peppercorns
½ teasp coriander seeds
1 bay leaf
freshly chopped parsley
½ teasp salt

Place all the ingredients except the mushrooms or courgettes and chopped parsley in an enamel or stainless steel pan. Simmer for 8–10 minutes and then throw in the mushrooms or courgettes. Simmer for 5–8 minutes. With a slotted spoon remove the mushrooms or courgettes while still crisp to a shallow serving dish and boil down the liquid until well flavoured and about ¼ pt (150ml) is left. Remove the bundle of herbs. Pour the liquid over the vegetables, chill and sprinkle with freshly chopped parsley.

** Tomatoes Stuffed with Cream Cheese and Herbs

This is a most delicious dish, the flavours blending admirably when carefully made with tasty fresh tomatoes.

Ingredients
4–6 people

4–6 fine ripe tomatoes
6 oz (175g) cream cheese (such as Eden
   Vale Somerset soft cream cheese)
1–2 tbs very finely chopped shallot
2 teasp fresh chopped or ¼–½ teasp
   dried basil
1 tbs finely scissored chives
½ teasp green peppercorns
4 fl oz (100ml) double cream ⎫
2 tbs plain yoghurt   ⎬ *or* use Crème Fraîche
chopped chervil or parsley   ⎭
salt
pepper (if necessary)

Cover the tomatoes with boiling water and leave for 30 seconds or so before plunging into cold water and peeling. Cut off the tops and remove the inner pulp carefully, especially around the stalk end. Salt lightly inside and leave upside down to drain for about ¼ hour.

Combine the cream cheese with the very finely chopped shallots, basil and chives. Stir in the green peppercorns and season with salt. Add 2–3 tbs of the cream to make a soft mixture. Drain and dry the tomatoes, fill with the cheese mixture and replace tops. Place on a serving dish and, just before serving, pour over the remaining cream, mixed until smooth with the yoghurt (or you can slightly acidulate the cream with lemon juice). Scatter with chopped chervil or parsley and serve.

*   # Cheesy Potatoes

I turn to this when I want a nice simple supper and there is not much around from which to make it. With good potatoes and fresh herbs it makes a tasty dish.

Ingredients
4–6 people

2 lb (900g) even-sized potatoes
fresh lemon thyme, thyme or dried
   Italian seasoning
plenty of scissored chives

Sauce
1 oz (25g) butter
1 tbs oil
1 large onion
14 oz (400g) tin tomatoes (4–8 fresh
   tomatoes)
2 fl oz (50ml) cream
4–6 oz (100–175g) grated strong cheese
salt and pepper

Boil the unpeeled potatoes in salted water until they are just cooked, then peel them and cut into quarters or thick slices. Lay them in a buttered gratin dish, scatter with chopped lemon thyme, thyme, or Italian seasoning, pour over the sauce, sprinkle heavily with scissored chives and serve.

Sauce. Heat the butter and oil and cook the chopped onion until golden and tender. Add the drained and roughly chopped tinned tomatoes (or peeled fresh tomatoes) and fry for about 5 minutes until tender and sauce-like. Stir in the cream, cheese and plenty of seasoning, heat gently, stirring, until the cheese has just melted, and pour over the potatoes.

F **   Little Mushroom Pies

These little pies are made with cream cheese pastry and a spiced mushroom filling for a nice first course, picnic dish or savoury. You can keep the uncooked pies or the prepared filling in the freezer.

Ingredients
1 dozen pies

Mushroom Filling

	Cream Cheese Pastry
½–¾ lb (225–350g) mushrooms	3 oz (75g) soft butter
1 oz (25g) butter	3 oz (75g) cream cheese
2–3 shallots or 1 finely chopped onion	6 oz (175g) plain flour
1 clove finely chopped garlic	good pinch salt
1 tbs plain flour	
4–5 tbs yoghurt, sour cream or cream	
dash tabasco sauce or cayenne pepper	
1 tbs finely chopped parsley	
a little chopped fresh or pinch dried lemon thyme or thyme	
freshly grated nutmeg	
squeeze lemon juice	
egg wash	
salt and pepper	

Cream Cheese Pastry. Cream the soft butter well, beat in the cream cheese, sift in the flour and salt and work to a dough. Knead briefly into a flat disc and rest in a plastic bag in the fridge for about ½–2 hours.

Mushroom Filling. Melt the butter in a frying pan and fry the finely chopped shallot or onion until softened. Slice and add the mushrooms, cutting the slices in halves or quarters if they are large, add the chopped garlic and fry over high heat until lightly cooked, the moisture has evaporated and the butter is again apparent (sometimes mushrooms in autumn can be very watery, and you have to remove them from the pan and boil the liquid away before returning them and continuing). Sprinkle over the flour and cook for a moment or two; then add the yoghurt, spoonful by spoonful, stirring all the time and letting it cook into the dish so that it does not curdle. Season with tabasco or cayenne, nutmeg, seasoning and chopped herbs, add a good squeeze of lemon juice and cook until thick and creamy. Cool the mixture.

Roll the pastry thinly and cut bottoms and lids to fit mince-pie tins. Lay in the bases and fill with a teaspoonful of the mushroom filling. Moisten lids round the edge with cold water and press in place. Prick the tops, brush with egg-wash and bake in a hot oven (400°F/200°C/Gas 7) for 15–20 minutes until crisp and brown. Serve hot or cold.

** Lady Farquhar's Beetroot Salad

This is an old recipe from my great-great-grandmother which I rather like. I usually cut the beetroot, once cooked, into 'chips' rather than slices, and the caraway is my addition. The recipe says that a few sliced potatoes may be added.

Ingredients
4–6 people

1–2 lb (450–900g) beetroot
3–4 tbs tarragon vinegar (or shallot
   vinegar)
½ teasp caraway seeds (optional)

Dressing
1 egg yolk
1 teasp Dijon mustard
1 teasp sugar
1–2 teasp Worcester sauce
2 tbs oil
3 tbs cream
1 teasp capers
salt and pepper

Boil the beetroot, unpeeled and with the leaf stump left on, in plenty of boiling salt water until tender and the skins rub off. Peel, slice (food processor with chipper blade), season and sprinkle with the vinegar and caraway seeds and leave to cool.

Dressing. Combine the egg yolk, seasoning, mustard, sugar and Worcester sauce, beat in the oil and cream and add the capers. Pour over the beetroot, toss and serve chilled.

*   Cold Beef and Potato Salad

Cold boiled or roasted meat, mixed with sliced cooked potatoes and dressed with a herby spicy vinaigrette dressing, is one of the best ways of using up the remains of the joint in summer.

Ingredients
4–6 people

10 oz (275g) or more cooked sliced beef
1 lb (450g) potatoes
1–2 tbs wine vinegar
watercress or lettuce leaves
2 oz (50g) black olives (optional)
salt and pepper

Dressing
1 shallot or small onion
1 tbs Dijon mustard
3 tbs fresh chopped parsley or mixed
    herbs (parsley, marjoram, chives,
    thyme, etc) or 1 teasp dried Italian
    seasoning soaked in 1 tbs boiling
    water for 5 minutes
2–3 tbs wine vinegar
6–8 tbs olive or groundnut oil
salt and pepper

Boil the potatoes in their skins, then peel, slice, season, sprinkle with vinegar and leave to cool (or use left-over boiled potatoes).

Cut the beef into strips, combine with the potatoes and dressing and toss all together well. Line a bowl with watercress or lettuce leaves, arrange the beef and potato salad on them and, if used, scatter with black olives.

Dressing. Finely chop the shallot or onion and combine with the mustard, plenty of salt and pepper, the chopped fresh herbs or soaked dried ones and their water. Stir in the vinegar, then gradually stir in the oil to make a thick dressing (or shake it all up in a tightly closed jar).

**   Spring or Autumn Salad

These vegetables are at their best in spring, though also available in autumn. The individual character of this dish comes from the use of hard-boiled egg to thicken the dressing and the use of fruit juice in place of vinegar (though you may need a drop or two of vinegar as well if the fruit is very sweet and lacks acidity).

Ingredients
4–6 people

½ small cauliflower
4 oz (100g) button mushrooms
1 bunch watercress
1 bunch radishes
2–3 small carrots (optional)
2 hard-boiled eggs

Dressing
salt
pepper
1 teasp French mustard
juice of ½ grapefruit or 1 orange
4 tbs olive oil

Break the cauliflower into small florets, blanch in boiling salted water for 2–3 minutes, refresh under the cold tap and drain. Wash and trim the watercress. Slice the mushrooms, radishes and carrots. Keep one egg yolk for the dressing and roughly chop the remaining egg and white. Arrange all attractively in a salad bowl. When ready to serve, dress and toss.

Dressing. Crush the egg yolk in a bowl with salt, pepper and mustard until smooth. Beat in 2–3 tbs fruit juice and then the oil.

** Gratin of Green Beans, Smoky Bacon and Mushrooms

When the French beans are getting larger, they can be used in this lightly bound gratin, flavoured with smoked bacon to make a good supper dish or to serve with cold meat.

Ingredients
4–6 people

1½ lb (675g) French beans
3 oz (75g) smoked streaky bacon, cut
    thick
4 oz (100g) field or button mushrooms
1½ oz (40g) butter
1 tbs potato flour
5 fl oz (150ml) cream or milk or a mixture
10 fl oz (300ml) bean cooking water
2 teasp finely chopped summer savory or
    parsley
4–6 tbs grated cheese
4–6 tbs breadcrumbs
salt and pepper

Toss the prepared beans into lightly salted boiling water and cook until just tender. Drain, reserving the cooking liquid.

Meanwhile, dice the bacon and fry in 1 oz (25g) butter until lightly golden (I use a wok or large frying pan which will eventually hold all the ingredients). Slice the mushrooms thickly, add, and sauté until just done. Mix the potato flour with the cream and/or milk, add to 10 fl oz (300ml) of the reserved bean cooking water and combine in the pan with the bacon and mushrooms. Bring to the boil, stirring, and simmer for 1–2 minutes. Stir in the cooked beans, seasoning and herbs, and toss to coat with sauce. Turn into a buttered gratin dish, top with grated cheese, breadcrumbs and flakes of butter and pop under the grill to brown. It can also be set aside and reheated in a hot oven (400°F/200°C/Gas 7) for about 30 minutes.

*   Goose or Duck Salad

A duck goes a long way if roasted and served cold in a salad. You can also use leftover duck or goose meat, particularly the thighs. This makes a pleasant fresh salad around Christmas, and the crispened strips of skin add a nice touch.

Ingredients
4–6 people

½–¾ lb (225–350g) cold cooked goose or
  duck
goose or duck skin (if available)
2 eating apples ⎫ *or* use 3 oranges
1 clementine, satsuma or orange ⎭
1 head celery or Chinese leaves

Dressing
1 teasp Dijon mustard
1 teasp red currant or mint jelly
1 tbs sherry *or* wine vinegar
good squeeze lemon juice
a little grated orange rind (optional)
3–4 tbs best olive oil
salt and pepper

Take any piece of goose or duck skin and cut into strips. Season highly and roast in a hot oven, or under the grill, for 3–5 minutes, until the fat renders out and the strips are crisp. Set aside to sprinkle over the salad.

Cut the meat into thumbnail dice. Core, quarter and cube the apple, and add de-pithed clementine segments or orange segments, cut out from the skin. Slice the celery or Chinese leaves.

Combine all the ingredients, season and toss with dressing. Scatter with crispy skin if available.

Dressing. Make the dressing by mixing the mustard, jelly and vinegar with the lemon juice, grated orange rind and seasoning. Mix well, and energetically stir in the oil to make a thick dressing.

*   # Christmas Salad

We often need salads at Christmas to go with cold meats and pies. This one is easy to prepare, is nice and crunchy and keeps well, so I usually make a big batch. You can also add hard-boiled eggs, diced turkey or ham if you want to make it into a main course salad.

Ingredients
4–6 people

1–2 eating apples
6 oz (175g) potatoes boiled in their skins
6–12 oz (175–350g) cooked beetroot
2 dill cucumbers (optional)
1 shallot or ½ very small onion
2–4 sticks celery or ½ head Florence
    fennel
6 oz (175g) thinly-sliced white cabbage
1–2 oz (25–50g) walnut halves
1–2 tbs vinegar
salt, pepper and sugar

Dressing
8 fl oz (225ml) mayonnaise
1 teasp paprika
1 teasp Dijon mustard
½ clove garlic
¼ teasp dried dill or dill seed
little vinegar to taste
1 small beetroot (optional)
salt and pepper

Core the apple. Dice the potatoes, beetroot, dill cucumbers and apple. Finely chop the onion and slice the celery or fennel. Turn with the sliced cabbage into a bowl and sprinkle with salt, pepper, a little sugar and the vinegar. Add the dressing and toss well. Serve scattered with the walnut halves.

Hard-boiled eggs, diced turkey or ham can all be added to this salad.

Dressing. Combine the mayonnaise with the paprika, mustard, pressed garlic and dill or dill seed. Add vinegar to taste and correct the seasoning.

If you wish, you can process a small beetroot in with the mayonnaise for a rose pink dressing, but don't over do it or it can be very lurid!

**   Oriental Rice Salad

This bright yellow mound of rice, flecked with green and red peppers and covered with crunchy brown almonds, looks great on a buffet.

Ingredients
4–6 people

8–12 oz (225–350g) long grain rice
1 teasp turmeric
½–1 teasp lime or lemon pickle (optional)
1 tbs vinegar
2–3 tbs oil
½ red pepper

¼ green pepper
1 small tin pineapple pieces
1 small tin drained sweetcorn
1 oz (25g) browned flaked almonds
salt and pepper

Boil the rice in plenty of boiling salt water, with the turmeric added, for 10–14 minutes until firm but cooked. Drain into a colander and rinse with cold water, shake well and drain for 10 minutes or so. Make a little dressing with the chopped lime pickle (if used), salt, pepper, oil and vinegar. Add the rice and mix well. You will find it needs only very little dressing. Stir in the diced peppers, bits of pineapple and sweetcorn. On serving scatter generously with the browned flaked almonds.

**   Spinach Salad with Anchovy and Croûtons

Spring is just the time for a spinach salad. The leaves will be delicious, tender and full of vitamins. I find Greenmarket a good variety to grow; it hasn't too powerful a flavour for eating raw but is excellent cooked. So many varieties are available now and some, like perpetual spinach, are rather coarse for salads, except when caught very young, but they are useful all-year standbys.

Ingredients
4–6 people

½–¾ lb (225–350g) young spinach

Dressing
8–10 anchovy fillets
1 teasp Dijon mustard
4 teasp wine vinegar
3–4 tbs fruity olive oil
1 tbs oil from the anchovies
plenty of pepper and very little salt

Croûtons
3 slices stale bread
½ oz (12g) butter
2 tbs fruity olive oil

Remove tough stalks and midribs from the spinach, wash and shake dry. Crisp in a sealed bag in the fridge if necessary.

When ready to serve, turn the salad into the dressing, add the croûtons, toss well and serve at once.

Croûtons. Heat the butter and oil in a frying pan, de-crust and dice the bread, add it to the hot fat and sauté until crisp and brown; keep warm.

Dressing. Chop the anchovy fillets into pieces and place in a salad bowl with salt, pepper and mustard. Add the vinegar, stir well to dissolve the salt and gradually whisk in the oils.

* Salade des Gourmets

Tiny fresh French beans bathed in a vinaigrette with chopped shallot and wafer-sliced pink baby mushrooms. A mouthful of a first course or a salad.

Ingredients
4 people

½ lb (225g) very young French beans
2 oz (50g) firm button mushrooms

Dressing
1 tbs finely chopped shallots
1 tbs white wine vinegar
3 tbs olive oil
salt and pepper

Toss the whole beans into a saucepan of boiling salt water, cook until still very crisp to the teeth, drain and refresh under the cold tap to set the colour. Combine the cold drained beans and very finely sliced mushrooms. Toss well with the dressing and serve well chilled.

Dressing. Mix together the salt, pepper, shallots and vinegar. Stir well and gradually beat in the oil.

✳✳   Gratin Dauphinois

There are many recipes for this, one school of thought saying categorically that there is *pas question de fromage*, another using Franche-Comté or Gruyère cheese. The wonderful thing about it is that it can be made quite simply with potatoes, milk and a bit of Cheddar; perhaps in that case it should only be called a Gratin de Pommes de Terre, but it accompanies Monday's cold meat admirably. This version, with that fine combination of garlic, nutmeg, cream and Gruyère which is wickedly lavish, cries out 'Eat me on my own, I'm so delicious'. It makes a feast with cold meats and salad.

Ingredients
4–6 people

2½ lb (1.15kg) peeled and thinly sliced
    potatoes (salad type are best)
½ pt (300ml) milk
1 clove garlic
2 oz (50g) butter
2 oz (50g) grated Gruyère cheese
¼ pt (150ml) double cream
salt, pepper and nutmeg

Rub a shallow gratin dish with the cut clove of garlic, then crush it, add it to the milk in a pan and heat. Generously butter the dish and put in a layer of the potatoes. Dot with butter, sprinkle with cheese and season with salt, pepper and a little freshly grated nutmeg. Continue the layers and finish with the cream and seasoning. Remove the garlic from the milk and pour carefully over, then sprinkle with the remaining cheese and dot with the last of the butter. Bake for about 40 minutes in a hot oven (400°F/200°C/Gas 6) until golden and tender.

   This dish will keep warm very happily and can be re-heated in a moderate oven (350°F/180°C/Gas 4); keep undercooked at the first cooking and do not let it dry out. You cannot prepare it and leave it aside to cook later as the potatoes will discolour.

F **   **Chou Rouge aux Marrons**

Long slow cooking makes this French winter dish. Very good with tinned chestnuts or even without any when you can't get them or can't face shelling them.

Ingredients
4–6 people

2 lb (900g) red cabbage
¼ lb (100g) very thick slices of streaky
    bacon
2 oz (50g) goose or pork fat or butter
2 large sliced onions
3 peeled and diced cooking apples
1 clove garlic
1 bay leaf
nutmeg
ground cloves

¼ pt (150ml) strong red wine
¼ pt (150ml) good stock
2–3 tbs wine vinegar
2 tbs redcurrant jelly
16–20 chestnuts
salt and pepper

Gently fry the diced bacon and onion in the fat in a large (preferably earthenware) casserole. Thinly slice the cabbage, removing the core, stir in and turn until every slice glistens. Add the apples, chopped garlic and bay leaf and season with pepper, nutmeg, ground cloves and plenty of salt. Pour over the wine, stock and vinegar and simmer for about 1½ hours on the stove or in a very moderate oven (325°F/170°C/Gas 3).

To skin chestnuts. I have tried every method and find this the best way. Cut halfway round the skin of the chestnuts on the rounded side and drop a few at a time into boiling water; boil for 3 minutes and remove one at a time to peel off the outer and inner skins together. If you get it just right you should be able literally to squeeze them and they will pop out of their shells.

Add the chestnuts to the cabbage with the redcurrant jelly and a little more stock if needed and cook slowly for another 1–1½ hours until the chestnuts are tender and the liquid all but gone. Correct the seasoning and serve.
    This dish reheats beautifully and often tastes even better on the second occasion.

**   **Winter Salad with Thousand Island Dressing**

We eat so many salads that it's nice to vary the dressings. This is one I'm always being asked for.

Ingredients
4–6 people

Thousand Island Dressing

1 small head white cabbage or Chinese
  leaves
3–4 sticks celery
2–3 eating apples
2–3 carrots
½ green or red pepper
1 oz (25g) sultanas plumped in a little
  warm water
1–2 oz (25–50g) walnuts
½ teasp carraway seeds
1–2 teasp sugar
1–2 tbs vinegar
salt and pepper

1 egg
½ teasp dry mustard
2 tbs wine vinegar
8 fl oz (225ml) olive, sunflower, peanut or
  mixed oil
1 teasp chilli sauce
1 slice onion
1 stick celery with leaves
2 tbs chopped parsley
½" (1–2cm) slice of green pepper
1 teasp paprika
½ teasp salt
pepper

Finely slice or shred the salad ingredients, add the sultanas and broken walnuts, season with salt, pepper, carraway, a little sugar and vinegar and fold in the Thousand Island Dressing.

Thousand Island Dressing. Break the egg into a food processor or liquidiser and add mustard, salt, pepper and vinegar. Switch on and gradually add the oil to make a mayonnaise. Add the remaining ingredients with the vegetables roughly chopped. Process until fairly smooth.

$\mathcal{P}$ *   ## Herring Salad

This salt herring salad from South Africa is useful because you can buy salt herrings from a delicatessen and keep them for a week or so in the fridge.

Ingredients
4–6 people

2 salt herrings (filleted and soaked for 24 hours in milk)
1 small mild onion
2 eating apples
2 large pickled dill cucumbers

3–4 tbs tomato ketchup
1 tbs tomato purée
1 tbs wine vinegar
1–2 tbs sugar
pepper

Fillet and soak the salt herring in milk for 24 hours. Drain and cut the fillets in small pieces, dice the apples and cucumber and slice the onion very finely. Combine the tomato ketchup, tomato purée, sugar, vinegar and pepper to make a dressing. Stir in the herring, apple and vegetables. Chill for 2–12 hours and serve as a first course or part of a mixed Hors d'Oeuvre. Diced potato and beetroot can also be added.

$\mathcal{P}$ **   ## Haricots Blancs en Salade

For those who appreciate the flavour of olive oil and beans, this rich dried bean salad will not last long. But do make sure you use beans which are fresh, preferably from a quick-turnover health food shop.

Ingredients
4–6 people

½ lb (225g) best white haricot beans
¼ pt (150ml) good fruity olive oil
2–3 cloves garlic
bay leaf
sprig of thyme

1 tbs tomato purée
1 lemon
a few spring onions, shallots or very finely chopped onion
salt and pepper

Toss the beans into a large saucepan of boiling water, boil 2 minutes, take from the stove and leave to soak for 1 hour, or else soak overnight in cold water.

Heat the oil in a saucepan or casserole, add the drained beans and simmer very gently for about ten minutes. Add the garlic, bay leaf, thyme and tomato purée. Cover by 1 inch (2–3cm) with boiling water and simmer over low heat or in a slow oven (300°F/150°C/ Gas 2) for about 3 hours until tender and the liquid has thickened to form a sauce. Squeeze over the lemon juice, season with salt and pepper, add the chopped onion and serve cold.

*   Coupe Juli

A fresh crunchy starter, excellent if you have a rich dish to follow. It can be done in individual dishes or glasses for easy serving.

Ingredients
4–6 people

some cauliflower florets
1–2 avocado pears (depending on size)
2 pears or ¼ small melon
4″ (10cm) cucumber

Dressing
½ teasp honey
½ teasp Dijon mustard
2 tbs lemon juice
6 tbs olive oil
1 tbs each of fresh, finely chopped chives,
   parsley and mint
salt and pepper

Toss the cauliflower florets into boiling salt water for 2 minutes to blanch, and refresh in cold water until chilled; drain well.

Dressing. Mix the salt, pepper, mustard and honey with the lemon juice, then gradually beat in the oil to make a dressing. Stir in the herbs. Peel and dice the avocado, pear (or melon) and cucumber and turn into the dressing with the cauliflower. Mix thoroughly and leave to chill for 2–4 hours, mixing once or twice.

Serve well chilled in individual glasses accompanied by Sesame Fingers or brown bread spread with anchovy butter and rolled up.

**   Tzatziki

I was shown this Graeco-Turkish dish of cubed cucumber with yoghurt in Cyprus by a dear lady who was supposed to clean my house. When I discovered she was a cook the dust was left to roll up and down the corridors while she taught me authentic dishes. This one is lovely as an Hors d'Oeuvre or salad and cool on the tongue with curries and hot peppery dishes. They put no pepper in it; it is our obsession to add salt and pepper to everything.

Ingredients
4–6 people

1 large cucumber
½–¾ pt (300–450ml) yoghurt
2 tbs olive oil

1–2 cloves garlic
1 teasp dried mint (*not* fresh)
salt

Remove about half the cucumber skin lengthwise in strips and cut all the cucumber into flattish dice. Cream the garlic with salt and add the yoghurt, beat in the olive oil and mint and stir in the cucumber. Check the taste and chill. Serve with kebabs or as an Hors d'Oeuvre.

If the yoghurt is very thin, strain it in muslin for ½ hour to remove excess liquid. If the cucumbers are bitter sprinkle the dice with salt, press, and leave to drain for 30 minutes.

** Beetroot Orange Salad

The orange dressing seems to bring out the full flavour of the beetroot.

Ingredients
4–6 people

1 lb (450g) beetroot
2 oranges
½–1 oz (12–25g) walnuts

2–3 tbs vinegar (sherry, cider or tarragon)
2–3 tbs walnut or olive oil
sugar, salt and pepper

Boil the beetroot until tender, skin and dice. While still warm, sprinkle with the vinegar and some grated orange rind. Season with salt, pepper and sugar. When cold add the walnut or olive oil and toss. Cut off the peel, pith and skin from the oranges and cut away the segments from their skin. Add to the beetroot. Sprinkle over the roughly broken walnuts and serve.

*   Salade Niçoise

This Provençal speciality can be assembled very quickly and merits being dressed with a good fruity olive oil.

Ingredients
4–6 people

1 crisp lettuce
1 small tin anchovies
¾ lb (350g) firm tomatoes
4 hard-boiled eggs
12–24 black olives (depending on size,
   but they should be the little olives of
   Provence)

Dressing
2 tbs wine or tarragon vinegar
1 clove garlic
8 tbs fruity olive oil
a little chopped chervil and tarragon
   (optional)
salt and pepper

Optional extras
8 oz (225g) French beans
3 oz (75g) tin tuna fish in oil
1 small thinly sliced shallot or mild onion
a few sliced boiled potatoes
sliced green or red pepper

If you are using French beans, blanch them in boiling water until done but still crisp; drain and refresh under the cold tap. Drain.

Place the lettuce in a large salad bowl or in individual bowls, rubbed with garlic, and arrange on it the quartered eggs and tomatoes (and beans, onion, pepper and potato if used). Scatter over the anchovies and olives and chunks of tuna (if used).

Dressing. Either flatten the clove of garlic under the blade of a knife, mix with the salt, pepper and vinegar, then beat in the oil and herbs and hand this dressing on serving the salad. Or add the herbs to the salad and let everyone season and drip over vinegar and oil to their taste. The main thing is that the salad must not be dressed or tossed until just before being eaten.

**   French Tomato and Rice Salad

Rice cooked and dressed while warm with a vinaigrette and with lots of chopped tomatoes added. It makes a lovely summer salad, but do not overdress or it becomes oily. When I lived with a French family it was always a picnic dish, taken along in a huge wooden bowl. I've always found it a great favourite.

Ingredients

4–6 people

8 oz (225g) long grain rice	*Dressing*
1 lb (450g) firm ripe tomatoes	2 tbs tarragon vinegar
1–2 tbs chopped chives	6 tbs olive oil
1–2 tbs chopped tarragon or parsley	salt, pepper and French mustard

Boil the rice in plenty of boiling salted water until just cooked but with some bite in it. Drain in a colander and rinse with cold water. Shake out all the surplus water and dress while still warm with some of the dressing. Pour boiling water over the tomatoes and leave for thirty seconds or until the skins are loosened; plunge into cold water, skin and chop roughly. Stir into the rice with the finely chopped fresh herbs and season well with salt and pepper, adding more dressing as necessary.

Dressing. Mix the salt, pepper and mustard with the vinegar, stir well to dissolve the salt, then beat in the oil.

* Dill Cucumber Salad

In Germany one so often gets this cucumber salad with a slightly sweet fresh dill and cream dressing.

Ingredients

4–6 people

1 large cucumber or several smaller garden ones	¾ teasp sugar
3 fl oz (75ml) cream	1 teasp wine vinegar
1 teasp chopped fresh or ¼ teasp dried dill	1 teasp oil
	salt and pepper

Peel and slice the cucumber, not too thinly, sprinkle with salt in a colander, lay a plate on top and press with a weight for ½ hour or so to expel the juices. Place salt, pepper, most of the dill, sugar and vinegar in a bowl and stir to dissolve the salt and sugar. Add the cream and whisk until it begins to thicken. Whisk in the oil, and check the seasoning. Pat the cucumber dry with kitchen paper and mix with the dressing. Turn into a dish and serve sprinkled with the rest of the dill. The dill flavour develops after a little while.

Variation. Use sour cream instead of fresh, or yoghurt and cream mixed.

Main Dishes

T **   **Alsatian Onion Tart**

Around Alsace you find a great variety of onion tarts; some are crispy pastry just spread with onions, others an inch or so deep with a creamy onion filling. All are delicious.

Ingredients
4–6 people

Pastry
8 oz (225g) flour
4 oz (100g) firm butter
about 4 tbs cold water
salt

Filling
4 oz (100g) thickly cut smoked bacon
1 oz (25g) butter
1½ lb (675g) onions
½ oz (12g) flour
8 fl oz (225ml) single or whipping cream
4 eggs
salt, pepper and nutmeg

Pastry. Sift the flour into a bowl or food processor with metal blade, add two pinches of salt and the firm butter in small pieces. Sprinkle over the water and mix with your fingertips or process until the pastry forms a ball. Knead briefly into a flat disc and rest for ½–2 hours in the fridge. Roll the pastry thinly to fit a 9" (24cm) flan tin, prick the pastry and line with tinfoil and gravel or beans, and bake in a hot oven (400°F/200°C/Gas 6) for 6–8 minutes or until the pastry is set. Remove the tinfoil and gravel or beans and pour the filling into the pastry case, sprinkle over the nutmeg and place in moderately hot oven (375°F/190°C/Gas 5). Bake for 15–25 minutes until the filling is just set.

Filling. Cook the diced bacon until crisp and remove from the pan; add the butter to the pan, fry the sliced onions for about 15–20 minutes or until soft and golden and season with salt and plenty of pepper. Take the pan off the stove, return the bacon and sprinkle over the flour; add the cream and mix well. Break in the eggs one by one, season and mix thoroughly.

F ** Koftas with Sunflower Seeds

Another light, cheap and easy dish enjoyed by children and the young is this Middle Eastern dish of meat balls in tomato sauce. It is especially delicious when made with lamb. The toasted sunflower seeds are nearly as good as the authentic, but astronomically priced, pine-kernels, and are much cheaper.

Ingredients
4–6 people

1 lb (450g) lean shoulder or leg of lamb or braising beef	*Sauce*
	2½ oz (60g) tomato purée
1 small finely chopped onion	¼ pt (150ml) water
1 egg	salt and pepper
2 oz (50g) white breadcrumbs	½ lemon
½ lemon	1–2 tbs sunflower seeds
2 tbs finely chopped parsley	
½ teasp pounded cummin	
½ teasp pounded coriander seeds	
3–4 tbs cold water	
plenty of salt and pepper	
oil or fat for frying	

With a Food Processor. Remove all gristle and sinews from the meat and chop finely, using the metal blade; then add the onion, egg, grated lemon rind, lemon juice, seasoning, herbs and breadcrumbs. Process to a smooth paste, adding cold water for lightness.

Without a Food Processor. Mince the meat finely, then blend with the other ingredients as above in a liquidiser until very fine and smooth.

With wet hands form into marble-sized balls and fry gently in a little hot oil until golden; shake the balls round the pan so that they brown all over. Pour off any excessive fat and add the sauce. Stir in the brown tasty bits from round the pan. Season lightly and simmer very gently uncovered for 20–30 minutes until the sauce is rich and reduced. You can also cook the meat balls in a moderate oven (350°F/180°C/Gas 4). Brown the sunflower seeds lightly in a drop of oil in a frying pan and scatter over the top of the meat balls on serving. Serve with buttered noodles or rice.

Sauce. Mix the tomato purée with lemon juice, seasoning and water.

*   Jambon Braisé au Madère

When you've seen enough of your lovely cold ham, carve some generous slices for this dish.

Ingredients
4–6 people

1½–2 lb (675–900g) thick slices of cold cooked ham
1 finely diced carrot
1 finely diced onion
3½ oz (85g) butter
¼ pt (150ml) Madeira

¼ pt (150ml) good stock
1 bay leaf
1 teasp–1 tbs potato flour or arrowroot
4 oz (100g) button mushrooms
salt and pepper

Melt 1 oz (25g) butter in a casserole and gently brown the carrot and onion. Lay the slices of ham on top of the vegetables, pour over the stock and Madeira, add the bay leaf and bring to the simmer on top of the stove. Cover and place in a slow oven (300°F/150°C/ Gas 2) for 30 minutes or longer. Slice and sauté the mushrooms in 1 oz (25g) butter.

Strain the hot liquid from the ham into a small saucepan, thicken lightly with potato flour mixed with a little water and bring to the boil, stirring all the time. Add the mushrooms, correct the seasoning and simmer for 1 minute. Draw off the stove and beat in the remaining 1½ oz (35g) butter to thicken and enrich the sauce. Pour over the ham slices and serve at once.

F **   Sardine Croissants

These are adapted from one of Robert Carrier's recipes. They are a useful stand-by in the freezer, either uncooked or cooked. They can go straight from freezer to oven and be on the table within fifteen minutes.

Ingredients
24 croissants for 4–6 people

Cream Cheese Pastry
6 oz (175g) soft butter
6 oz (175g) curd or cream cheese
10 oz (275g) flour
¼ teasp salt

Sardine Filling
1 tin sardines
¼ teasp curry paste or powder
1 tbs finely chopped parsley
½ lemon
salt and pepper

Cream Cheese Pastry. Cream the butter and cheese well, using a wooden spoon or the food processor, then sift in the flour and salt and mix to a dough. Knead briefly into a flat disc and chill for 1 hour.

Roll the pastry thinly and cut into 4" (10cm) squares, then across into triangles. Put a teaspoonful of sardine filling in the centre of each triangle and roll up from base to point. Twist the ends to form into a crescent shape. Bake in a moderate oven (350°F/180°C/Gas 4) for 10–15 minutes until golden brown. Serve sizzling hot or take cold on picnics.

Sardine Filling. Add the curry, seasoning and parsley to the drained sardines and mash well, adding lemon juice to taste.

F * ## Haddock Monte Carlo

A delicious dish for any entertaining, but as it is quick to make I am putting it here. Freeze only unbaked, or your cheese will go rubbery.

Ingredients
4–6 people

1–1½ lb (450–675g) smoked haddock
   fillets
½ lb (225g) tomatoes
pepper

Sauce
1 oz (25g) butter
1 oz (25g) flour
¼ pt (150ml) milk
¼ pt (150ml) single or whipping cream
2–3 oz (50–75g) grated Gruyère cheese
salt, pepper and mace

Skin the haddock fillets and lay in one layer in a well buttered shallow baking dish. Skin, de-seed and dice the tomatoes and scatter over the fish. Season with pepper only. Pour the sauce over. Sprinkle with the grated cheese and bake uncovered in a moderately hot oven (375°F/190°C/Gas 5) for about 20 minutes. Brown under the grill if necessary.

Sauce. Melt the butter, add the flour and cook for 2–3 minutes over moderate heat, stirring. Draw off the stove, wait for the sizzling to cease and add the milk and cream. Bring to the boil, whisking with a wire whisk, and simmer for 1–2 minutes. Season with pepper, mace and very little salt. It should be a fairly thick coating sauce as some moisture will come out of the fish in the cooking.

F **   A Good Fish Pie

Good fresh fish, cooked and folded in large chunks into a parsley sauce and topped with creamy mashed potatoes. It freezes extremely well as long as you leave out the hard-boiled egg.

Ingredients
4–6 people

1–1½ lb (450–675g) cod, haddock or coley
   fillets
¾ pt (450ml) milk
2 oz (50g) butter
2 oz (50g) flour
2 hard-boiled eggs (optional)
2–3 tbs finely chopped parsley
1 bay leaf
mace
salt and pepper

Potato Topping
1½ lb (675g) potatoes
1–2 oz (25–50g) butter
milk
salt and pepper

Skin the fish fillets while raw (so much easier than picking over when hot), using a flexible knife and working from the tail with a horizontal sawing motion. Cover the fish with the milk, season with salt, pepper and mace and add a bay leaf. Bring to the simmer gently and cook for about 5–10 minutes until the fish will just flake. Strain, and when cool break into large flakes.

Melt the butter in a saucepan, add the flour and cook over moderate heat for 2–3 minutes. Take off the heat and leave until the sizzling has stopped. Strain in the cooking liquid from the fish, whisk well and bring to the boil. Simmer for 2–3 minutes, then carefully fold in the large flakes of fish, the roughly chopped eggs and plenty of parsley. Check the seasoning, turn into a buttered dish and top with creamy mashed potatoes. Brown under the grill or re-heat in a moderately hot oven (375°F/190°C/Gas 5) for about 35–45 minutes until brown and bubbling.

Potato Topping. Peel the potatoes and cut to even size. Boil gently in salted water until tender, drain and press through a potato ricer or crush well with a potato masher or fork. When smooth draw aside and add some milk and butter to the bottom of the pan. When warm, beat in over the heat until you have a smooth purée. Season well.

P ** **Spiced Pork**

There are many variations of this dish. This is based on one of Elizabeth David's recipes, and I find it invaluable and economical. We have fed twenty-five ladies off a 5½ lb (2.5kg) hand. Get your butcher to skin and bone the pork. I sometimes spice and freeze it all ready to cook when it comes out of the freezer.

Ingredients
12–20 people

4–6 lb (1.8–2.7kg) skinned and boned
   hand of pork
skin and bones from the pork
10–12 juniper berries
1 tbs sea salt
1 teasp peppercorns
½ teasp cummin seed
1 clove garlic
2 bay leaves
2 fresh or dried fennel stalks or ½ teasp
   seeds
2 slices lemon
½ pt (300ml) dry white wine or cider as
   second best

Pound together the salt, peppercorns, cummin, garlic and juniper berries in a mortar and rub well into the meat. Tie the joint in a good roll, tucking the leg bit into the hole, and lay in a tight-fitting casserole with the skin underneath and the bones around it. Tuck in the bay leaves, lemon slices and fennel stalks or seeds and leave in a cool place for 12–24 hours. Add the wine and enough water to cover the meat, cover with greaseproof paper or tinfoil and a tightly-fitting lid and cook in a slow oven (275°F/140°C/Gas 1–2) for 4–6 hours until well done and soft when prodded with a skewer. Leave to cool in the stock, then take out and dry well if you are not using for a day or two. Keep in the cool. Serve thinly sliced with baked or sauté potatoes and salads. Strain the stock, which should be very good, clear and jellied; it makes delicious soups or sauces. Any fat from the top will be tasty for frying.

P ＊   # Herring Fillets in Lemon Cream

When fresh herring are in, this dish of raw filleted fish in a lemon cream dressing can be made a day or two ahead and is most unusual and popular.

Ingredients
4–6 people

2–3 fine herrings
1/3 pt (200ml) double cream
1 lemon
3 tbs olive oil
3–4 tbs white wine vinegar
1 very finely sliced small onion
2 peeled, cored and diced sharp apples
2 bay leaves
salt and pepper

Fillet the fish (or get the fishmonger to do so) and cut first into strips and then into bite-sized pieces. Season very well with salt and pepper. Whisk the cream lightly, adding grated lemon rind, juice, vinegar and oil. Stir in the onion, apple and whole bay leaves and season well. Fold in the herring bits and turn into a serving dish. Cover and marinate in the fridge for 24–48 hours before serving cold with brown bread and butter.

F ＊   # Mince with Herby Cheese Crumble

A great favourite, this freezes well ready-made but unbaked, or it can be whipped up fairly quickly from scratch. Freeze your mince in thin layers the size of a handkerchief, separated by cling film, and they will prise apart and thaw quite quickly.

Ingredients
4–6 people

1–1½ lb (450–675g) mince
2 oz (50g) dripping
1 finely chopped onion
2 diced carrots
1 finely chopped stick celery
1½ oz (35g) flour
½ pt (300ml) stock
2 teasp Worcester sauce
1 teasp mushroom ketchup
salt and pepper

Herby Cheese Crumble
6 oz (175g) flour
1½ oz (35g) butter
1½ oz (35g) grated cheese
plenty of freshly chopped parsley and
    other herbs
salt, pepper and paprika

Melt half the dripping in a casserole or saucepan and gently cook the finely chopped vegetables. Heat the remaining dripping in a frying pan and brown the mince fast over high heat (cook in several batches). Add to the vegetables and stir in the flour, seasoning and stock. Cook for ½–1 hour (depending on your mince) in a moderate oven (350°F/180°C/Gas 4) until tender. Or it can simmer on top of the stove. Turn into a pie dish and cover with the crumble. Bake for 30 minutes in a moderately hot oven (375°F/190°C/Gas 5) until the top is brown.

Herby Cheese Crumble. Rub the butter into the flour. Add the grated cheese, chopped herbs and seasoning.

*   Potato and Ham Gratin

Layers of sliced potato and chopped ham topped with cheese make this an easy bake which will wait for you.

Ingredients
4–6 people

2–2½ lb (900g–1.15kg) potatoes
¾–1 lb (350–450g) cooked ham
¼ lb (100g) button mushrooms
1 clove garlic
2 oz (50g) butter

½ pt (300ml) milk
¼ pt (150ml) cream
2–3 oz (50–75g) Gruyère or strong Cheddar cheese
salt, pepper and nutmeg

Rub a flat gratin dish, preferably earthenware, with a cut clove of garlic and butter liberally.

Place the crushed garlic in a saucepan with the milk and bring to the simmer. Grate the cheese and put on one side. Slice the mushrooms and set aside. Cut the ham into small slices or strips. Slice the potatoes thinly (a food processor makes this child's play). Layer the potatoes in the prepared dish with the ham, the mushrooms, a seasoning of very little salt, pepper and a scrape of nutmeg; dot with butter and sprinkle with a little grated cheese. Continue these layers, finishing with potato. Pour over the hot milk (without the garlic) and the cream and top with grated cheese and dabs of butter. Bake for about 40 minutes in a hot oven (400°F/200°C/Gas 6) until golden and tender.

$\mathcal{PF}$ ✳✳   # Lasagne Vincigras

This lasagne dish is very rich, unusual and delicious. Freeze only uncooked, since once cooked the cheese goes rubbery.

Ingredients
4–6 people

½ lb (225g) lasagne or home-made pasta
    using 6 oz (175g) flour
½–1 oz (12–25g) dried cèpe mushrooms
1 finely chopped onion
4 oz (100g) chicken livers
4 oz (100g) chicken breast (raw or cooked)
2 oz (50g) butter
1 teasp tomato purée
½ pt (300ml) good stock
¼ teasp ground cinnamon
2 tbs Marsala
3 oz (75g) freshly grated Parmesan cheese
salt and pepper

White Sauce
2 oz (50g) butter
2 oz (50g) flour
1 pt (600ml) milk
salt and pepper

Topping
¼ pt (150ml) milk
1 oz (25g) Parmesan cheese
nutmeg

Soak the mushrooms in a little warm water for half-an-hour or so. Sauté the diced chicken breast and the diced livers, which have first been carefully picked over to remove any green-tinged flesh, in 1 oz (25g) butter and set aside. Add the remaining butter to the pan and gently fry the onion until golden. Add the chopped mushrooms (add their water to the stock but watch for sand at the bottom) and ¼ pt (150ml) stock, and simmer to reduce for 10 minutes. Stir in the tomato purée, season and add the remaining stock. Simmer for a further 15 minutes, then stir in the meat, cinnamon and Marsala. You should now have a rich syrupy brown sauce, but reduce further if necessary before adding half the white sauce. Simmer for 10 minutes.

White Sauce. Melt the butter in a saucepan and add the flour. Cook over moderate heat, stirring, for 2–3 minutes, then draw off the stove, wait until cooled a little, add the milk and bring to the boil, whisking with a wire whisk. Simmer for 2–3 minutes and season with salt and pepper.

Topping. Add the milk to the remaining white sauce together with the Parmesan cheese and nutmeg and set aside, covered, to top the dish.

To assemble. Cook the lasagne for 15–18 minutes (3–5 minutes for home-made pasta) in boiling, salted water until *al dente*. Drain and rinse with cold water. Butter a gratin dish well and layer the meat sauce, lasagne and grated Parmesan, seasoning each layer as you go. Top with the reserved white sauce, cover and set aside overnight (not essential). Bake in a moderate oven (350°F/180°C/Gas 4) for ¾–1 hour and serve when golden and bubbling.

ℱ ✳✳   Farthinghoe Country Quiche

I don't know many recipes for wholemeal pastry that I find work very well. This one does, and I use healthy granary flour to give it taste and texture and a good nutty crunch. The filling is a country mixture of smoked bacon, cheese and mushrooms, but vary this as the spirit moves you. You can also use it to make cooked tartlets filled subsequently, perhaps with cold chicken and vegetables in mayonnaise.

Should you wish to make the pastry with a soft, sunflower oil margarine you must use it really well chilled or frozen so that you don't make too soft a dough, for this pastry needs to include enough water so that it won't be crumbly when cooked.

Ingredients
4–6 people

Pastry
3½ oz (85g) firm butter or margarine
6 oz (175g) granary flour
½ teasp salt
4 tbs cold water

Filling
3–4 oz (75–100g) smoked streaky bacon, cut thick
½ oz (12g) butter or margarine
4 oz (100g) mushrooms (optional)
3 eggs *or* 2 eggs and 2 yolks
6 fl oz (175ml) milk and 4 fl oz (100 ml) cream *or* use all milk
3–4 oz (75–100g) Cheddar cheese
1–2 tomatoes (optional)
salt, pepper and nutmeg

Pastry. If using soft margarine and a food processor, cube the margarine and chill in the freezer until firm. If you are making the pastry by hand, freeze the margarine, then grate into the flour quickly.

Place the flour and salt in a bowl, or in the food processor with metal blade, and add firm butter or frozen margarine in cubes or grated. Rub in or process, adding the water at once, until a dough forms; knead briefly until smooth, then form into a flat disc and chill for ½–2 hours until firm. Roll very thinly and line a 9″ (24cm) flan tin; prick the base and line with tinfoil and baking beans. Bake in a hot oven (425°F/220°C/Gas 7) for 8–12 minutes until set; then remove tinfoil and beans and continue to bake in a moderately hot oven (375°F/190°C/Gas 5) for a further 10–15 minutes until firm but not too brown. Fill with the filling and continue to bake for about 20–30 minutes until the filling is just firm and golden brown. Serve at once, while the pastry is crisp. The quiche is also nice warm or cold, and it freezes very well.

Filling. Cut the bacon into large dice and fry in the butter until lightly browned. Add the mushrooms, if used, and sauté lightly. Beat together the eggs, milk and cream, seasoning and three-quarters of the cheese, add the bacon and mushrooms and pour into the quiche. Top with sliced tomato, if used, and sprinkle over remaining cheese.

*   # Kedgeree

Whether it is for breakfast or for supper, made with salmon or smoked haddock, kedgeree is a firm favourite. It is one of those dishes adopted from India which has really stuck, even if it has lost its original spices and is now made with fish rather than lentils. The quantities don't have to be too precise so long as the rice does not swamp the fish and you are generous with the butter.

It might be useful to know that 1 lb (450g) of raw fillet gives you about 9 oz (250g) of cooked, flaked fish. Each ounce of uncooked rice will weigh about 2½ oz (65g) when cooked, so use about 7½ oz (210g) of uncooked rice for this recipe.

Ingredients
4–6 people

9 oz (250g) cooked flaked salmon or
  smoked haddock
1¼ lb (550g) cooked rice
3–4 oz (75–100g) butter

2–3 hard boiled or soft boiled eggs
1 egg
2–3 tbs finely chopped parsley
salt and cayenne pepper

Melt the butter in a large frying pan and, when hot, add the rice, flaked fish and roughly chopped eggs. Toss and turn until hot through, seasoning with salt and cayenne to taste; it should be fairly highly seasoned. Then toss in most of the parsley. Make a little nest and break in the egg; cover it with the hot rice and leave to cook gently for about half a minute. Stir the semi-cooked egg right through the kedgeree and serve at once whilst moist, sprinkled with the reserved parsley.

Chopped onion fried in the butter, chives, curry powder or a little cream can all be added with advantage to vary the kedgeree.

F **   # Fish Cakes

Salmon, haddock, cod or coley all make good fish-cakes. They are lovely for breakfast, and rather a treat these days, or good for lunch or supper. It is worth making them in quantity and freezing. The balance of fish, potato and seasoning is the important thing.

Ingredients
10–12 fishcakes

1–1½ lb (450–675g) raw or ¾ lb (350g)
  cooked and flaked salmon, haddock,
  cod or coley
¾ lb (350g) mashed potato
3 tbs mixed chopped chives and parsley
2–3 eggs

seasoned flour
2–3 drops oil
approx 3–4 oz (75–100g) dried
  breadcrumbs
salt and pepper
fat or oil for frying

Cook the fish in a little seasoned milk if raw; skin and flake.

Mix the flaked fish and mashed potato, add seasoning and herbs and bind with one of the eggs. Form into cakes with floured hands and pat with seasoned flour. (The fish cakes can be fried just like this if time is short, but they won't be so crisp.) Whisk the remaining eggs with a few drops of oil to help give a crisp crust, and a pinch of salt to break down the egg. First dip the fish cakes into the egg, then roll them in breadcrumbs until well coated.

Heat about ¼"–½" (½–1cm) fat or oil in a frying pan and, when hot, fry the fish cakes briskly on each side to a nice brown. Drain on kitchen paper and serve.

Having formed the cakes, I often chill them until firm in the freezer because they are then easier to dip in the egg and breadcrumbs.

Chicken Liver Scalpicon

Here we lightly sauté chicken livers and serve them in a tasty sauce. They can be served in little cocottes on their own, with rice, or on toast, or can be used to fill vol-au-vents, pastry shells and pancakes.

Ingredients
4–6 people

¾–1 lb (350–450g) chicken or duck livers
2 oz (50g) butter
1 finely chopped onion
4 oz (100g) mushrooms or
    1 tbs mushroom ketchup (optional)
¾ oz (20g) plain flour
5 fl oz (150ml) red wine or 2–3 tbs
    Madeira or sherry   } to make up to 15 fl oz (450 ml)
10 fl oz (300ml) good stock
1 teasp tomato purée
1 tbs finely chopped parsley
salt, pepper and cayenne

Pick the chicken livers over, carefully removing threads and green-tinged flesh which can be bitter. Cut into generous pieces.

Melt the butter and gently fry the onion. When soft but not brown, turn up the heat and fry the chicken livers and mushrooms (if used), halved or quartered if large, until the livers are sealed and lightly browned but still rosy inside. Remove from the pan and add the flour to the butter in the pan. Cook gently for 2–3 minutes, remove from the heat, wait for the sizzling to cease and add the wine (or Madeira or sherry), stock and tomato purée (and the mushroom ketchup if used). Bring to the boil, whisking, and simmer for 10–20 minutes until reduced and rich looking. Season and return the chicken livers and mushrooms to the sauce, together with the chopped parsley. Serve on toast.

** Ham and Banana Rolls au Gratin

Ingredients
4–6 people

8 slices ham
2 large bananas
10 fl oz (300ml) milk, heated with 1 slice
     onion and several sprigs rosemary
1 oz (25g) butter
1 oz (25g) plain flour

5 fl oz (150ml) whipping cream
1 teasp Dijon mustard
squeeze lemon juice
1–2 oz (25–50g) grated cheese
salt and pepper

Heat the milk with the onion and rosemary and leave, covered, to infuse for about 10 minutes.

Melt the butter in a saucepan, add the flour and cook, stirring, over moderate heat for 1–2 minutes. Draw the pan off the heat, wait for the sizzling to cease, then add the strained, flavoured milk. Bring to the boil, whisking well, and simmer for 1–2 minutes. Thin with the cream, add mustard, very little salt but plenty of pepper and a squeeze of lemon juice.

Cut the peeled bananas in half lengthways and again in half cross-ways; wrap each slice of ham round a piece of banana and place in a well-greased gratin dish. Cover with the sauce and scatter with the cheese. Bake in a moderately hot oven (375°F/190°C/Gas 5) for 25–35 minutes until bubbling and golden.

* Bacon Stovies

A slightly more elaborate version which can be used as a supper dish, especially nice if you can get some proper old-fashioned cured and smoked bacon. Meat or ham in larger quantities or grated cheese can be layered with sliced potatoes and fried onion for endless variations; the important things are the heavy tightly-lidded pan (some say it should be iron) and gentle heat.

Ingredients
4–6 people

1½–2 lb (675–900g) peeled even-sized
     potatoes
4 oz (100g) thick cut smoked bacon
2 tbs dripping, fat or oil

2 large sliced onions
4 fl oz (100ml) water
finely chopped parsley
salt and pepper

Dice the bacon and melt the dripping in a heavy casserole; add the bacon and onion and cook until the onion softens and the bacon browns a little. Cut the potatoes into generous chunks or leave them whole. Add them to the pan, mix them in, season and add the water. Cover closely and cook over very gentle heat for 30–40 minutes, until the potatoes are soft and tender and probably rather broken up, and the liquid has gone. Sprinkle with parsley and serve from the pan.

** Cheese Soufflé

You must have well-flavoured cheese for a soufflé, because if you just add a larger quantity of bland cheese it will become too heavy.

I cook soufflés more slowly than chefs who are working 'on command' and therefore wish to get them to their ready-seated customers as soon as possible. Cooked in this way they stay at perfection for longer than if cooked fast, allowing you a little more leeway to get them to the table.

Ingredients
4–6 people

¾ pt (450ml) milk
½ bay leaf
1 slice onion
1 blade mace
2 oz (50g) butter
1½ oz (35g) flour

4–6 oz (100–175g) grated cheese
    (half-Gruyère, half-Parmesan is best,
    or good mature Cheddar)
5 egg yolks
6 egg-whites
salt, pepper and mustard

Heat and infuse the milk with the onion, bay and mace. Melt the butter in a saucepan, add the flour and cook over moderate heat for 2–3 minutes, stirring. Draw off the stove, wait for the sizzling to cease and add the strained milk. Bring to the boil, whisking hard, and simmer 1–2 minutes. Add the cheese, stir until it melts and add the seasoning. Remove from the heat, cool a little and beat in the egg yolks. Whisk the whites until just holding a peak and gently fold into the warm cheese mixture.

Turn into a 2 pt (1.2l) soufflé dish, well buttered, especially around the rim. Smooth the top carefully to the edges and cook in a moderate oven (350°F/180°C/Gas 4) for 30–40 minutes, until well risen, golden and just trembling in the middle when you move the dish. Serve immediately; the outside should be set but the centre should still be like creamy sauce.

F **   # Spiced Sausage Turnover

This will keep hot, wrapped in many layers of newspaper and tinfoil, for 3–4 hours, and is a great favourite for shooting and winter picnics. It can be prepared and left ready to cook for a large party, and is especially popular with teenagers. If you want to freeze it, use fresh sausage-meat and fresh pastry and omit the hard-boiled egg. Freeze uncooked and allow a little longer cooking time.

Ingredients
4–6 people

½ lb (225g) pkt puff pastry
1 lb (450g) best pork sausage-meat
½ oz (12g) dripping or oil
1 finely chopped onion
2–3 oz (50–75g) mushrooms (optional)
2 peeled, de-seeded and diced tomatoes
1 tbs chopped fresh or ¼ teasp dried
    herbs
1–2 hard-boiled eggs
1 egg
salt, pepper and ground mace

Melt the dripping or oil in a small frying pan and soften the onion in it. Halve or quarter the mushrooms (if used), add, and fry for 3–4 minutes. Add the mixture to the sausage-meat with the tomatoes, chopped herbs and roughly cut up hard-boiled eggs. Mix well together, binding with an egg and seasoning with salt, pepper and mace.

Roll the packet of pastry thinly to a square of approximately 12″ × 12″ (30cm × 30cm). Trim off the edges with a sharp knife and cut off a ½″ (1cm) strip for decoration. Set on a greased baking sheet and place the sausage-meat mixture down the centre; fold up both sides of the pastry and seal with water in a zig-zag crest along the top. Decorate with pastry trimmings, cut 1–2 slits to let the steam out and brush with egg wash. Bake in a hot oven (425°F/220°C/Gas 7) for 30 minutes or so until well risen, crisp and golden. Serve at once, cut into generous slices, or wrap up for a picnic.

$\mathcal{F}$ **   **Asparagus and Ham Quiche**

Ingredients
4–6 people

12 oz (350g) fresh asparagus
4 eggs (or 3 yolks + 2 eggs)
2 fl oz (50ml) whipping cream
3 oz (75g) diced ham
¼–½ oz (6–12g) butter
salt and pepper

All-Purpose Pastry
1 egg yolk and about 2 tbs cold water *or*
  3–4 tbs cold water
6 oz (175g) plain flour
3 oz (75g) firm butter
a good pinch of salt

All-Purpose Pastry

By hand. If you are using a yolk, mix it with the 2 tbs cold water. Sift the flour and salt into a wide mixing bowl and add the firm butter cut into hazelnut-sized pieces. Rub in the butter, sprinkling over the yolk and water mixed, or just water, as you work, and pinching the whole lot into a dough. When formed into a rough dough turn out on to a board, and with the heel of your hand smear the pastry down the board in egg-sized lumps finally to amalgamate it. Knead briefly into a flat disc. Rest in a plastic bag in the fridge for 1–2 hours or overnight.

In the Food Processor. Sift the flour and salt into the bowl of the food processor with the metal blade in place, add the firm butter cut into hazelnut-sized pieces and have your yolk and cold water, or just cold water, ready. Switch on, and add the yolk and water at once; process until the mixture just draws together into a lump. Turn out on to a board and smear down the board in egg-sized lumps (though I hardly feel it needs this *fraisage* when made in the food processor). Knead briefly into a flat disc. Rest in a plastic bag in the fridge for 1–2 hours or overnight.

Roll the pastry and line a 9" (24cm) removable base flan tin. Prick the base, line with tinfoil and baking beans and bake in a hot over (400°F/200°C/Gas 6) for 8–10 minutes; then remove the tinfoil and continue to bake in a moderately hot oven (375°F/190°C/Gas 5) for about 15 minutes until lightly golden and almost cooked, covering lightly with tin foil if the rim seems to be getting too brown.

Cook the asparagus in the minimum of lightly salted water, tying thicker stalks into a separate bundle from the thinner spears and cooking for longer. Drain, reserve the water, and set 8–12 tips aside for garnish. Roughly chop the remainder, discarding tough stalks and purée, adding a little of the reserved water. When very smooth, put through a fine sieve and make up to 10 fl oz (300ml) with some of the reserved asparagus water.

Whisk the eggs and add the asparagus purée, cream and seasoning. Scatter the diced ham over the pastry shell, pour over the asparagus mixture, decorate with reserved asparagus tips and dot with butter. Bake in a moderately hot oven (375°F/190°C/Gas 5) until just set right through. Serve hot, warm or cold.

**   Courgette and Smoked Ham Quiche

If you have no time to de-gorge the courgettes, wring them out in a tea towel to expel their excess moisture. This combination of flavours is most successful and makes a good hot or cold quiche.

Ingredients
4–6 people

Filling
¾–1 lb (350–460g) small courgettes
4 oz (100g) smoked ham or smoked
   sausage
1 oz (25g) butter
1 tbs olive oil
1 large chopped onion
3 eggs
4 fl oz (100ml) cream *or* mixture of cream
   and milk
1 teasp chopped fresh or good pinch
   dried marjoram
2–3 oz (50–76g) grated Cheddar cheese
salt and pepper

All Purpose Pastry
1 egg yolk and about 2 tbs cold water *or*
   3–4 tbs cold water
6 oz (175g) plain flour
3 oz (75g) firm butter
good pinch salt

Pastry. If you are using a yolk, mix it with the cold water. Sift the flour and salt into a bowl or food processor with metal blade, add the firm butter, cut into hazelnut sized cubes, and rub in or process, adding the yolk and water as you go, until a pastry forms. If not thoroughly combined, turn the pastry on to a board and smear it down the board in egg sized lumps with the heel of your hand (*fraisage*) finally to amalgamate it. Knead briefly into a flat disc and rest, in a plastic bag, in the fridge for ½–2 hours. Roll and line a 9" (24cm) flan tin with the pastry, prick the base lightly with a fork, line with aluminium foil and baking beans and cook in a hot oven (400°F/200°C/Gas 6) for about 10 minutes. Remove the foil and baking beans, lower the temperature to 375°F/190°C/Gas 5 and continue to cook for 10–15 minutes longer before adding the filling.

Filling. Slice the courgettes and layer in a colander, sprinkling each layer with salt. Press with a plate and weights and leave to de-gorge for 20 minutes or so before draining off all the expelled water and patting dry on kitchen paper.

   Meanwhile heat the butter and oil in a frying pan and fry the onion until soft and golden. Turn up the heat, add the drained courgettes and sauté over fierce heat for several minutes until just beginning to brown. Layer the prepared pastry case with the sliced or diced ham or sausage and the courgette filling. Whisk the eggs with the cream or milk and cream, seasoning and marjoram, and pour over the filling. Scatter with grated cheese and bake in a moderate oven (350°F/180°C/Gas 4) until the filling has set. Serve hot, warm or cold.

F ** Pork with Cider and Apple or Quince

It's a very old and good custom to cook pork with apple. This makes an extremely nice casserole, especially if you can use quinces or just include a small proportion of quince.

Ingredients
4–6 people

1½–2 lb (675–900g) boned shoulder of
   pork
2½ oz (65g) pork fat, dripping or butter
1 tbs oil
2 sliced onions
2 tbs calvados or brandy
1 oz (25g) flour
8 fl oz (225ml) dry cider
8 fl oz (225ml) stock
bouquet garni of parsley stalks, sage and
   bay leaf
1 clove garlic
2 teasp paprika
4 medium cooking or eating apples or
   quinces or quince and apple mixed
salt and pepper

Remove the skin from the pork and cut the meat into 1½" (4cm) cubes. Cut some of the pork skin into very fine dice to add later to give richness to the dish.

Heat the oil and half the pork fat, dripping or butter in a large frying pan and fry the onions until soft. Add the pork cubes and fry until they are lightly browned on all sides and the onion is brown. Flame with calvados or brandy, sprinkle with flour and toss. Turn into a casserole and de-glaze the pan with cider and stock. Add to the casserole with the cubes of pork skin, the flattened clove of garlic and the bouquet garni, paprika and seasoning.

Meanwhile melt the remaining fat or butter in a frying pan and add the peeled, cored and thickly sliced apple or quince. Fry until light golden on each side, then add to the casserole. Cover and simmer gently or cook in a slow oven (300°F/150°C/Gas 2) for 1½–2 hours until the pork is absolutely tender and the sauce rich and tasty.

This dish tastes even better re-heated, and freezes beautifully.

𝓕 ** Spiced Fish Turnovers

Little spicy fish parcels in a cheesy flaky pastry are greatly enjoyed when handed round hot with drinks. They also make a nice first course or savoury. They will freeze and can be cooked from frozen, and any left-over filling is nice cooked under a baked egg.

Ingredients
36 turnovers

Filling
12 oz (350g) haddock fillet
½ pt (300ml) milk
1 bay leaf
1½ oz (35g) butter
1 small finely chopped onion
2 teasp curry powder
1 oz (25g) plain flour
1 egg yolk
pinch ground mace
black pepper
egg wash

Cheesy Flaky Pastry
8 oz (225g) plain flour
6 oz (175g) firm butter
2 oz (50g) grated strong cheese
3–4 tbs iced water
½ teasp dry English mustard
a little black pepper
good pinch salt

Cheesy Flaky Pastry. Sieve the flour into a bowl or the food processor with the salt, pepper and mustard. Add the grated cheese and firm butter, cut into hazelnut-sized cubes. Rub in, or process, as you add the water, and stop the moment the mixture draws together. Lightly knead together and roll out on a well-floured board to an oblong 10″ × 5″ (25cm × 12cm). Brush off excess flour, fold the top third down and the bottom third up and give the pastry a turn to the right. Roll and fold the pastry twice more, then rest in a plastic bag in the fridge for 1–2 hours.

Roll the pastry very thin and cut out 36 or so 3″ (8cm) circles of pastry. Place a small spoonful of cold filling on each round, moisten the edges with water, fold over and seal the pastry together to form turnovers. Brush with egg wash, make a tiny slit in the top, and bake in a hot oven (425°F/220°C/Gas 7) for about 15 minutes until crisp and golden. Serve piping hot.

Filling. Place the skinned fish in a saucepan with the milk, bay leaf, a turn or two of pepper and a pinch of mace. Bring to the simmer and cook gently until the fish will just flake. Drain and reserve the liquid.

   Melt the butter in a saucepan, add the onion, curry powder and another pinch of mace and cook gently until soft and golden. Off the stove, stir in the flour, egg yolk and cooled fish milk all at once. Whisk and just bring to the boil. Fold in the flaked fish and correct the seasoning; the mixture should be fairly stiff and highly seasoned. Turn out on to a plate, cover and leave until cold.

ℱ ** **Pork Italian**

Osso Buco is so good, but as it is not always possible to get veal shank I have evolved this dish, which uses tender shoulder of pork with the characteristic blend of tomato, garlic, anchovy and lemon that is the signature of *osso buco*. I serve it with either saffron rice or Risotto Doré.

Ingredients
4–6 people

2–2½ lb (900g–1.15kg) shoulder of pork
1 oz (25g) seasoned flour
2 tbs olive oil
2 oz (50g) butter
2 finely chopped onions
2–3 tbs tomato purée
14 oz (400g) tin tomatoes, drained
¼ pt (150ml) dry white wine
2 cloves garlic
¼ pt (150ml) stock
2–4 anchovy fillets
salt and pepper

To Serve

3 tbs parsley	finely chopped
grated rind ½ lemon	together to make
1 clove garlic	a *gremolata*

Heat the oil and butter together in a frying pan. Cut the meat into 1½" (4cm) cubes, toss in the seasoned flour and brown in the heated oil and butter. Remove the meat to a casserole and add the onion to the pan. Fry until lightly browned, then add the tomato purée and fry for 1–2 minutes. Add the roughly chopped tomatoes and the wine and boil hard for 3–4 minutes. Pour this sauce over the meat, season, and add the flattened garlic and the stock. Cover and cook very gently in a slow oven (300°F/150°C/Gas 2) for 2–3 hours or until very tender. Half-an-hour before serving, add the chopped anchovy fillets.

To Serve. Remove the meat and boil down the sauce if it's not already thick and rich. Serve on a bed of saffron rice and sprinkle heavily with the *gremolata* of finely chopped parsley, lemon rind and garlic.

P ** **Lincolnshire Stuffed Chine**

This stuffed collar of bacon was a traditional dish for Trinity Sunday. It makes use of fresh herbs, including young blackcurrant leaves, which give a delicious fragrance to the stuffing, and young raspberry leaves, which add a certain dry astringency. It is very easy to prepare and simple to cook, eats extremely well cold and is a perfect example of a dish which makes the most of what's around at a certain time of year but which nowadays could easily be lost. Make it any time from when the first young leaves appear in April till they get a bit tough in mid June. I also simply cook a ready-rolled joint of bacon, on a good bed of herbs, in a parcel like this, at any time of year to give the bacon an interesting flavour.

Ingredients
8–12 people or more

4 lb (1.8kg) piece of smoked collar of
    bacon (the whole piece would weigh
    up to 8 lb (3.6kg) if you want to do it
    for a party)
3–4 spring onions
5–6 tender lettuce leaves
good handful parsley
2–3 sprigs thyme
2–3 sprigs marjoram (or less of the
    annual one)
5–6 young blackcurrant leaves
2–3 young raspberry leaves

Soak the bacon for 2–3 hours or overnight as recommended by your butcher.

Chop together the spring onions, lettuce leaves, herbs and blackcurrant and raspberry leaves. Undo the strings on the bacon and open it up. Cut a few slits or pockets on the inside and spread with the herb mixture. Re-tie with string in several places (the larger piece you do, the easier it is to tie). Place the bacon on a double sheet of tinfoil on a roasting tin, cover it with another double sheet and fold the edges together to make a parcel (it used to be done in a flour and water pastry, but I find tinfoil is the modern answer). Bake for 25 minutes for each pound (450g) and 30 minutes over in a hot oven (400°F/200°C/Gas 6).

Leave until cold in the tinfoil parcel, then remove strings and skin before serving thinly sliced.

P *   ## Escabèche of Mackerel

Pickling fish to enhance its flavour and help it to keep has always been part of a cook's skill. The word escabèche intrigues me because one finds it with so many variations all round the world. Heavily pickled dishes to keep a great while are found in old books. Hanna Glasse in the eighteenth century has a recipe for pickled mackerel called *caveach*, and Meg Dods, the eminent Scottish cook of the early nineteenth century, has a recipe for *Cabeached Cod* which she says comes from the Spanish word escabèche, and means fish pickle. The escabèche crossed the Atlantic to become the Mexican Zeviche or Ceviche, changing to become uncooked fish, lightly pickled in lime or lemon juice.

   Nowadays we don't need to preserve for quite so far ahead, and can get away with a lighter pickle, much more to today's taste. But how useful it is, especially in summer when you may not feel like cooking, to be able to dip into a dish of pickled fish or, perhaps for week-end visitors, to prepare a dish several days before you need it.

Ingredients
4–6 people

4–6 fine mackerel
a little flour
8 fl oz (225ml) oil
1 sliced onion
1 diced carrot
8 fl oz (225ml) white wine vinegar
2 fl oz (50ml) water
several sprigs thyme
3–5 cloves garlic
½ bayleaf
2–3 parsley stalks
3–4 whole allspice
6–8 peppercorns
2 cloves
1 blade mace, or good pinch ground
     mace
salt and pepper

Gut the mackerel and cut off the head and tail. Cut each fish into 3–4 pieces through the backbone. Season, dip in flour, brush off the excess and fry in the hot oil, turning once, until brown and just cooked; remove to a deep dish. Add the onion, carrot, vinegar, water, thyme, garlic (either flattened under the blade of a knife or chopped small), bay leaf, parsley stalks, allspice, peppercorns, cloves, mace and 1 teasp salt to the oil in the pan; boil together for 5–10 minutes, then pour over the mackerel to cover. Cool, cover and keep for at least 24 hours before eating. It will keep for a week or so—longer if you salt the fish before cooking it.

Ŧ ** Cannelloni con Funghi

Ingredients
4–6 people

Spinach or Plain Pasta
10–12 oz (275–350g) plain strong flour
1 egg and 1 egg-yolk
2 oz (50g) spinach purée
½ teasp salt

or

8–12 squares of green lasagne

Filling
12 oz (350g) cooked ham, chicken, veal or
   pork
8 oz (225g) mushrooms
2 tbs olive oil
1½ oz (35g) butter
1 large finely chopped onion
1–2 tbs finely chopped parsley (flat
   leafed for choice)
3–4 tbs of the cheese sauce
salt and pepper
a little extra grated Parmesan

Cheese Sauce
2 oz (50g) butter
1½ oz (35g) flour
1 pt (600ml) milk
1–2 oz (25–50g) freshly grated Parmesan
salt, pepper and nutmeg

Spinach or Plain Pasta. If you do not use the spinach add another egg and one teasp olive oil. Mix all the ingredients to a firm dough and knead for 8–10 minutes until the dough is elastic and smooth. Alternatively, process all together in a food processor for 45 seconds, keeping the mixture (by the addition of more flour if necessary) in polystyrene-like granules. Then press together into a dough. Divide the dough into 3 pieces if rolling by hand and roll as thin as possible; otherwise divide into 4–6 pieces and pass through the pasta machine to the thinnest but one setting. Cut into 3″ × 4″ (8cm × 10cm) rectangles. Flour lightly and keep on a cloth on a tray if you are not yet ready to cook it.

   Boil the pasta squares in plenty of boiling salted water, with a few drops of oil added, until *al dente*; this takes 2–4 minutes for fresh or 10–15 minutes for dried pasta. Drain, rinse with cold water and keep in the minimum of cold water until ready to use.

Cheese Sauce. Make the sauce next so that it has time to mature while you make the filling. Melt the butter in a saucepan, add the flour and cook over moderate heat, stirring, for 2–3 minutes; then draw the pan off the stove and, when the sizzling has ceased, add the milk. Return to high heat and bring to the boil, whisking hard. Add the Parmesan and season with salt, pepper and nutmeg. If possible, leave over very low heat to mature for half-an-hour.

Filling. Cut the meat into small dice. Heat the oil and butter in a large frying pan, add the onion and cook gently until soft. Turn up the heat, slice the mushrooms and add. Sauté the mushrooms and, when nearly cooked, add the meat and sauté until hot through. Add the parsley, seasoning and 3–4 tbs of the sauce to bind the filling.

To Assemble. Butter a large gratin dish. Remove the pasta from the water, dry and fill with some of the filling. Roll up and place side by side in the dish. Cover with the remaining sauce and scatter with the extra Parmesan. Bake in a moderately hot oven (375°F/190°C/ Gas 5) until brown and bubbling; this takes 10–15 minutes if hot or 30–40 minutes if re-heating from cold.

ℱ ** Lasagne al Forno

A dish of baked lasagne is always very popular but can be quite a business to make with all its different components. So I have written a recipe for more than the usual quantity, either enough to feed 8–10 generously or to make two smaller dishes, one for now and one for the freezer. 'No-cook pasta' (packets of bought pasta that are supposed not to need cooking before baking) is a boon when you are in a hurry, but not as good as home-made, bought fresh or dry pasta cooked before assembling.

Ingredients
8–10 people

1 batch home-made spinach or plain
   pasta (*see page 108*) or 12 oz (350g)
   'no-cook' or packet lasagne
2–3 oz (50–75g) freshly grated Parmesan
   or rather more Cheddar

Meat Filling
4–8 oz (100–225g) diced salami
8 oz (225g) diced cooked ham
1 lb (450g) diced cooked chicken or cold
   roast meat
or use
1¾–2 lb (775–900g), or a
proportion, of raw beef mince
1–2 tbs olive oil
1 oz (25g) butter
1 large onion
2 cloves garlic
½–1 teasp freshly grated nutmeg
¼–½ teasp ground allspice
¼ teasp chilli or cayenne pepper
4 fl oz (100ml) dry white wine
salt and pepper

Tomato Sauce
1 × 1 lb 14 oz (850g) tin tomatoes
2 large onions
1 carrot
1 stick celery
2 cloves garlic
3 tbs olive oil
1 oz (25g) butter
4 oz (100g) tomato purée
8 fl oz (225ml) stock *or* water and ½
   chicken stock cube
1 bay leaf
salt and pepper

White Sauce
4 oz (100g) butter
4 oz (100g) plain flour
1½ pts (900ml) milk plus a little extra
freshly grated nutmeg
salt and pepper

Start with the tomato sauce, which should simmer for an hour or so; next prepare the meat and make the white sauce; lastly cook the lasagne (or soak the 'no-cook' lasagne) and assemble the dish.

Tomato Sauce. Finely chop the onions, carrot, celery and garlic and soften in the butter and oil, without browning, for about 10 minutes. Add the tomato purée and fry for several minutes before adding the roughly chopped tomatoes with their juice and the stock, bay leaf and a light seasoning. Simmer for about 1 hour until well reduced and tasty.

Meat Filling. Chop the onion and fry in the butter and oil in a wide pan for about 10 minutes until golden. Add the chopped garlic, diced salami, ham and cold meat (or beef mince) and sauté, stirring frequently, for 5–10 minutes until browning. Add the nutmeg, allspice, chilli and the wine with a light seasoning of salt and pepper. Simmer uncovered for 10–15 minutes or until almost all the liquid has gone. If using all raw minced beef add a little water and cover the pan, for the meat will need to cook until tender.

If using a mixture of raw and cooked meats, fry and simmer the raw meat, then sauté and add the cooked meats 10–15 minutes before the end of the cooking time.

White Sauce. Melt the butter in a saucepan, add the flour and cook, stirring, over moderate heat for 2–3 minutes. Draw the pan off the stove, wait for the sizzling to cease and add the milk. Bring to the boil, whisking hard, and simmer for 3–4 minutes. Season with nutmeg, salt and pepper and leave, covered, on the side of the stove to mature.

Lasagne. Cook the lasagne in plenty of boiling salted water with a tablespoon of oil added. The secret is to 'post' the lasagne in gradually, keeping the water boiling. If it stops, the pasta sulks on the bottom and sticks together. Cook home-made or fresh bought pasta for 3–5 minutes until just *al dente* (firm to the bite), or packet pasta for 15–20 minutes. 'No-cook' pasta is best thrown into boiling salted, oiled water just to soften and become flexible. Drain and rinse in cold water and keep in the minimum of cold water until ready to use (easier than spreading it on cloths all over the kitchen).

To Assemble. Butter a 9″ × 14″ (24cm × 36cm) gratin dish. Mix the meat filling with half the tomato sauce and 2–3 good tablespoons of the white sauce. Place a layer of plain tomato sauce over the bottom of the dish to stop the pasta from sticking. Layer with a quarter of the cooked, drained, lasagne, then cover with one third of the meat. Sprinkle with Parmesan and add the next layer of lasagne. Continue until you have four layers of lasagne and three of filling and cheese. Now pour the remaining tomato sauce over the lasagne and top the dish with the white sauce and a good sprinkle of Parmesan. Bake in a moderately hot oven (375°F/190°C/Gas 5) for ½–¾ hour until brown and bubbling. Alternatively, leave to stand for 12–24 hours, then bake in a moderate oven (350°F/180°C/Gas 4) for 1–1¼ hours until brown and bubbling.

Puddings

✳✳ Crème Brûlée or Burnt Cream

Another old English pudding, rich in cream and egg yolks and with a caramel top.

Ingredients
4–6 people

¾ pt (450ml) double or whipping cream
5 egg yolks
1½ oz (35g) vanilla sugar

½ vanilla pod
a few drops vanilla essence
castor sugar

Place the cream and vanilla pod in an enamel or stainless steel saucepan and bring very gently to the simmer, stirring occasionally to prevent scorching. Beat the vanilla sugar gradually into the egg yolks and continue to beat for 4–5 minutes until thick, pale and forming a 'ribbon'. Very slowly, drop by drop, beat the hot cream into the yolks. Add a few drops of vanilla essence and strain the custard into a 1-pt (600ml) soufflé dish, place the dish in a tin of hot water and bake in a very moderate oven (325°F/170°C/Gas 3) for about 45 minutes until set. Cool thoroughly and chill, then clean carefully round the edges.

Several hours before serving, heat the grill until very hot. Sprinkle ¼" (½cm) layer of castor sugar evenly over the top of the cream, especially up to the edges, and place high under the grill until the sugar has browned and turned to caramel; watch that it does not burn. Serve cold. It should have a hard shiny brown top.

Many household cookers simply will not heat evenly or hot enough, even when pre-heated for ½–¾ hour, to caramelise the sugar to a good brown without beginning to melt the cream. So the answer is to make a little caramel separately in a pan, using about 4 oz (100g) sugar and 2–3 tbs cold water, and pour it carefully over the top. It will harden very quickly.

F * # Peaches in Raspberry Sauce

This is one of the best puddings in the world, and it looks fabulous on a buffet. It is not difficult to make, but for eating standing up whole peaches can be a bit tricky to manage, and you may want to halve them.

Ingredients
4–6 people

4–6 large peaches
6 oz (175g) castor sugar
¼ pt (150ml) water

8 oz (225g) fresh or frozen raspberries
juice of ½ lemon

Dissolve the sugar in the water and boil for 2–3 minutes to form a syrup. Pour boiling water over the peaches and peel them. Poach the peaches gently in the syrup until tender, and remove to a serving dish to cool. Purée the raspberries with some of the cold syrup, sieve and sharpen with lemon juice. Pour over the peaches several hours before you want to eat them, and serve chilled.

To prepare ahead. The peaches can be poached several days ahead but keep them submerged in the syrup in a cool place. Don't put too many into one container or the bottom ones come out looking squashed. Purée the raspberries on the day and mix with only enough syrup to make a thick sauce.

F * # Rhubarb and Fresh Ginger Fool

Of the fruity puddings, this one fits the spring bill, but you do need nice pink sticks of rhubarb. I once used greenish sticks and the pudding ended up sludge brown-green, not very appetising, showing me how slightly wrong ingredients can completely change and often spoil a dish.

Ingredients
4–6 people

1½ lbs (675g) good pink rhubarb
1″ (2–3cm) fresh root ginger

6–8 oz (175–225g) sugar or to taste
⅓ pt (200ml) double cream

Cut the rhubarb into 1″ (3cm) lengths and cook with the skinned and grated ginger, the sugar and a drop of water until tender. Purée the rhubarb without its juice and cool. Whip the cream until it holds its shape, fold into the cold rhubarb purée, add a little more grated ginger or sugar if necessary and turn into a bowl or individual glasses. Serve with sponge fingers or little biscuits.

** Strawberry Soufflé

In summer use garden-fresh berries or in winter pots of strawberry purée from the freezer.

Ingredients
4–6 people

1 lb (450g) strawberries or ½ pt (300ml)
   purée
3 oz (75g) castor sugar or to taste
juice of ½ lemon
1 tbs (½ oz pkt) gelatine

3 tbs cold water
½ pt (300ml) cream
3 egg whites

Tie an oiled greaseproof collar round a 1 pt (600ml) soufflé dish. Sprinkle the gelatine on to the cold water in a cup, leave to soak for several minutes, then stand in a pan of hot water to melt. Purée the strawberries with the sugar and lemon juice and add the melted gelatine. Fold in the cream, whipped until just holding its shape, followed by the egg whites whipped until they too just hold a peak, and turn into the prepared soufflé dish. Chill 3–4 hours or more before serving.

Melted gelatine added to a very cold purée can set very quickly or even go stringy, so have your cream and egg whites ready whipped, your gelatine quite warm and your strawberry purée not too icy cold (though the best flavour is achieved from barely thawed berries). If made too far ahead, the enzymes in the strawberry seem to react with the gelatine and it may thin out.

F ** Soufflé au Citron

Lemon soufflé is often served, but this does not mean that it's still not one of the very best puddings. This version is sharp and tangy and not too firmly set.

Ingredients
4–6 people

3 eggs
4 oz (100g) sugar
2 lemons (5 tbs juice)
grated rind of 1 lemon

1 tbs (½ oz pkt) gelatine
3–4 tbs water
⅓ pt (200ml) cream
some flaked browned almonds

Sprinkle the gelatine on to the water in a cup and leave to soak 4–5 minutes. Stand in a saucepan of hot water until dissolved. Put the egg yolks, lemon juice, rind and sugar (all but one tablespoonful) in a bowl standing over a pan of hot water and whisk for 5–10 minutes, until thick, pale and golden. Remove and whisk 5 minutes more with the bowl standing in iced water. Whisk the cream until just holding its shape. Whisk the egg whites to a soft peak and beat in the remaining sugar. Add the gelatine to the yolks, then fold in the cream followed by the whites. Pour into a glass bowl or soufflé dish and chill. Decorate with flaked browned almonds.

This is just firm enough to stand up if placed in a soufflé dish with an oiled paper collar which is then peeled off when the soufflé is set. But it won't bounce round your plate like an india-rubber ball!

P *   Prunes in Claret

Do not despise a bowl of huge and shiny black prunes in a rich wine syrup for deep midwinter. These wrinkled fellows are far removed in flavour and size from our nursery memory, and are greatly appreciated with a jug of thick pouring cream.

Ingredients
4–6 people

1 lb (450g) best large prunes
¾ pt (450ml) water (approx)
1 vanilla pod
1 lemon

3 oz (75g) sugar
¼ pt (150ml) red wine (claret for choice)

Soak the prunes in the cold water with the grated rind of a lemon and the vanilla pod for 12–24 hours. Add the sugar and cook very gently for twenty minutes. Add the wine and continue to simmer until the prunes are very soft and the juice syrupy and delicious. Pour into a glass dish and serve chilled with cream.

** Marsala Oranges

Sliced oranges covered in a caramel Marsala syrup make a fine end to any meal.

Ingredients
4–6 people

4–6 good juicy oranges (placed in the
  fridge for 3–4 hours to make peeling
  easier)
8 oz (225g) granulated sugar

4 fl oz (100ml) cold water
5 fl oz (150ml) boiling water
5 fl oz (150ml) Marsala
1 lemon

Take julienne strips of rind from 1–2 of the oranges, using a julienne stripper or potato peeler and a knife to cut the pithless rind into matchsticks. Place in plenty of cold water and bring to the boil. Boil for 5–10 minutes until no longer bitter, then drain and refresh under the cold tap to set the colour.

In a heavy pan combine the sugar and cold water. Stir over gentle heat until the sugar has quite dissolved, then turn up the heat and boil without stirring to a good caramel brown. Still on the fire, add the boiling water but stand back—it spits like mad! The caramel will dissolve in water, giving you a caramel syrup. Add the Marsala, lemon juice and orange julienne and simmer down until you have a heavy syrup. Cool.

Cut the peel, pith and skin from all the oranges with a very sharp or serrated knife. Slice the oranges, removing any pips, and either re-form and stick together with a toothpick or place the slices in a serving dish. Add to the syrup any orange juice that has escaped, and pour over the oranges. Serve well chilled.

PF * Gooseberry Fool

The fruit is carefully cooked for flavour, then half-puréed and half-crushed to make an interesting texture. It's extravagant on cream, I know, but good, quick and easy.

Ingredients
4–6 people

1 lb (450g) gooseberries
4–6 oz (100–175g) sugar to taste
2 tbs water

½ pt (300ml) double cream
2–3 scented geranium leaves (optional)

Place the topped and tailed gooseberries and geranium leaves in a jar with the water and 3 oz (75g) sugar. Stand the covered jar in a pan of boiling water and let the water boil (or put in a slow oven) until the fruit pulps. Drain in a sieve. Crush one third and set it aside. Purée and sieve the remainder and combine with the crushed fruit. Sweeten and cool. Whip the cream fairly stiffly and fold in the cold gooseberry mixture. Turn into a serving dish and chill for 24 hours.

** Caramel Soufflé

The taste of this one belies its cost. It is easy to make, looks good and is a recipe everyone should know for using up those spare egg whites. But it does not freeze successfully.

Ingredients
4–6 people

4 egg whites
2½ teasp gelatine
3 tbs cold water
¼ pt (150ml) single or whipping cream

Caramel Syrup
8 oz (225g) granulated sugar
4 tbs cold water
¼ pt (150ml) boiling water
½ lemon

Caramel Syrup. Place the sugar and cold water in a heavy pan. Heat gently, stirring until every grain of sugar has completely dissolved. Turn up the heat, boil fast without stirring until it is a good dark caramel brown, and add the boiling water (watch out, it splutters like mad, but the caramel all dissolves in a moment). Cool, add the grated rind and lemon juice and pour into a measuring jug.

Sprinkle the gelatine on to the cold water in a cup and leave to soak for 3–4 minutes. Stand the cup in a pan of hot water to dissolve the gelatine and then cool a little. Whisk the egg whites until holding a peak and fold in the gelatine, followed by three-quarters of the cooled caramel syrup. Turn into an oiled 2 pt (1.2l) soufflé dish, chill and leave to set.

Turn out the soufflé by running a knife round the inside of the bowl and dipping the bowl in hot water for a few moments. Dry the bowl, cover with a serving dish and invert with a shake. If the soufflé does not come out, wrap a wrung-out hot cloth around the bowl and it should relent! Pour round the remaining caramel mixed with the cream, and serve.

*   Pêche or Poire Délice

A quickly whisked-up mixture to spoon over fresh or drained tinned fruit.

Ingredients
4–6 people

**4–6 fresh peaches or pears (or tinned in
    emergency)
2 tbs thin honey
2–3 tbs rum
¼ pt (150ml) double cream
a squeeze of lemon juice
a few browned flaked almonds**

Place the honey and rum in a bowl and stir until the honey dissolves (thick honey can be warmed with the rum, then cooled). Add the cream, whisk until the mixture is softly whipped, add a squeeze of lemon juice and spoon carefully over the peeled and sliced fruit in individual glasses. Top with a few flaked almonds.

F *   Chocolate Baked Pears

Pears baked in chocolate syrup, good hot or cold. A useful stand-by from the freezer.

Ingredients
4–6 people

**4–6 cooking or firm eating pears   ½ vanilla pod
4 oz (100g) vanilla sugar   2 oz (50g) plain eating chocolate
¼ pt (150ml) water   ½ oz (12g) butter**

Dissolve the vanilla sugar in water with the vanilla pod, then bring to the boil and boil for 5 minutes. Remove the vanilla pod. Slip in the peeled, cored and quartered pears and simmer until nearly done. Place the broken-up chocolate in a small bowl over hot water and when soft gradually stir in some cooled pear liquid and the butter. Pour back over the pears and continue cooking very slowly until the pears are done. Serve with ice cream or whipped cream.

* Rice Pudding Brûlé

The cheating instant pudding that can always be yours with the aid of a tin of rice pudding, brown sugar and a grill!

Ingredients
4–6 people

2 x 14-oz (400g) tins creamed rice pudding
soft dark brown sugar

Heat the grill. Turn the rice pudding into a shallow dish which it almost fills. Cover with a good ¼" (½cm) layer of sugar and put under the grill at once (or the sugar may dissolve) until bubbling and caramelised in parts. Serve at once, hot on top and cold underneath, or leave to cool.

* Spiced Peach Crumble

A sugar and spicy crumble scattered over drained peaches and cooked for almost instant success.

Ingredients
4–6 people

2 lb (900g) tin sliced peaches
5 oz (125g) flour
4 oz (100g) brown sugar
4 oz (100g) butter

2 oz (50g) Jordan's Original Crunchy or toasted oatflakes
grated rind of 1 lemon
¼ teasp ground cinnamon or mixed spice

Place the drained peaches in a buttered pie dish and sprinkle with a little cinnamon or mixed spice.

Rub the butter into the flour, sugar, grated lemon rind and cinnamon or spice until it resembles large breadcrumbs. Or mix in the food processor with plastic blade. Stir in the Crunchy and scatter on top of the peaches. Bake in a moderate oven (350°F/180°C/Gas 4) for 20–30 minutes until brown and bubbling.

*   # Ice Cream Ecossais

Scoops of bought ice cream with a little something added for style.

Ingredients
4–6 people

1 block of best dairy ice cream or 1 pt (600ml) home-made vanilla ice cream	4 tbs honey 4–6 fl oz (100–175ml) whisky

Very gently warm the honey and mix with the whisky. When it is well mixed cool. Scoop the ice cream into chilled glasses and pour the honey whisky sauce round it. Serve with wafers or biscuits.

ᖴ **   # Rhubarb Ice Cream

A delicately flavoured ice cream that I first came across in June in a rather nice restaurant in Alsace. I was confused by its soft pistachio green colour, but this is how it turns out late in the season, made with unforced sticks of rhubarb.

Ingredients
4–6 people

1½ lb (675g) rhubarb (pink rather than
    greenish for choice)
8 oz (225g) sugar or to taste
1–2 tbs water
½ pt (300ml) milk
3 egg yolks
8 fl oz (225ml) whipping cream

Cut up the rhubarb and stew with the sugar and 1–2 tbs water until tender. Drain and purée (you should have approximately 12 fl oz (350ml) of rhubarb purée). Cool.

Heat the milk. Whisk the egg yolks and gradually pour the hot milk on to them, stirring. Return to a double saucepan (not aluminium, which discolours egg yolks) or heavy pan and heat gently, stirring all the time, until the egg yolks thicken and the custard coats the back of a spoon. Do not let it boil. Cool.

Combine the cooled custard with the cold rhubarb purée and the cream. Pour into shallow metal or tinfoil containers and freeze, stirring in the edges once or twice as they freeze. When firm, process in the food processor or beat well until smooth. Re-freeze. Or make in an ice-cream machine. Mellow in the fridge before serving.

F * # Iced Mango Cream

A quickly made but most delicious pudding that just needs chilling well, or it can be frozen and thawed before serving.

Ingredients
4–6 people

14-oz (400g) tin mangoes   1 lemon
½ pt (300ml) double cream

Strain the mangoes, purée, and sieve to remove the fibres. Whip the cream and gradually beat in the mango purée and lemon juice to taste. Turn into individual pots or glasses or a bowl and freeze for several hours before serving lightly frozen, accompanied by little biscuits.

F * # Brown Bread Ice Cream

Ingredients
4–6 people

4 oz (100g) coarse, stale breadcrumbs from   3 oz (75g) vanilla sugar
    wholemeal or granary loaf   2 tbs brandy
1½ oz (35g) butter   6 tbs Crème de Cacao or Crème de Noyau
2 oz (50g) brown sugar   or rum
½ pt (300ml) cream

Melt the butter in a wide frying pan, add the breadcrumbs and toss and turn over moderate heat until they begin to brown. Add the sugar and continue to fry and stir until brown and caramelised (this takes a while). Remove from the heat. Whip the cream, adding the vanilla sugar, brandy and Crème de Cacao, turn into a tinfoil container or bowl and freeze until it starts to thicken. Fold in the cooled crumbs and freeze.

   Allow up to 1 hour to mellow in the fridge before serving. Hot chopped ginger in syrup is very good with this ice cream.

F ✳✳   ## Apple Chartreuse

Masses of apple slices baked for an unusually long time in a soufflé dish are then turned out to make an amber-coloured gâteau. Simple but unusual, and nice when you want a pure fruit sweet.

Ingredients
4–6 people

3 lb (1.35kg) apples (cookers, or eaters that keep their shape)
about 5–6 oz (125–175g) sugar to taste
¼ teasp mixed spice
4–5 tbs quince jelly or apricot jam

Caramel
4 oz (100g) granulated sugar
3 tbs cold water

Caramel. Dissolve the sugar in the water in a small pan over gentle heat, stirring. Once every grain of sugar has dissolved stop stirring, turn up the heat and boil fast to a good brown caramel. Pour at once into a warmed 1½–2 pt (900ml–1.1l) soufflé dish and coat the bottom and sides with the caramel.

Peel, core, quarter and slice the apples. Layer them with the mixed sugar and spice in the soufflé dish until full, pressing well down. Cover with a butter paper and bake (standing the dish in a pan of hot water to come halfway up) in a hot oven (400°F/200°C/Gas 6) for 2½–3 hours. Cool, and when lukewarm turn out on to a serving dish and spoon over the jelly or jam. Serve cold with cream.

F ✳✳   ## Spiced Pears

A pretty dish of whole pears in a spiced and lemony syrup. Pears freeze extremely well and are available most of the year.

Ingredients
4–6 people

6–8 pears
8 oz (225g) sugar
¼ pt (150ml) water

1 lemon
2 cloves
¼ stick cinnamon

Take julienne strips of lemon rind and blanch in boiling water for 10 minutes. Melt the sugar in the water and boil for 1–2 minutes; add the lemon juice, julienne strips, cloves and cinnamon. Peel the pears, leaving on the stalks, and poach in the syrup until tender. Remove the pears to a bowl, boil down the syrup until very heavy, remove the cloves and cinnamon and pour over the pears. Serve well chilled with thick cream.

F *   **Boodle's Orange Fool**

This is a speciality of the famous London club.

Ingredients
4–6 people

8" (20cm) home-made sponge cake
2 large oranges
1 lemon
2–3 oz (50–75g) castor sugar
½ pt (300ml) cream

Line a glass bowl or 2-pint (1.2l) soufflé dish with a thin layer of sponge. Whip the cream, adding sugar to taste, and the grated orange and lemon rind, and gradually drip in the orange and lemon juice. Pour into the sponge-lined bowl. Chill for at least 4 hours to allow the juice to flavour and thicken the cream and soak into the sponge.

** Soufflé Glacé

The recipe for this simply made frozen soufflé can be adapted to practically any liqueur.

Ingredients
4–6 people

3 egg yolks
2 eggs
4 oz (100g) castor sugar
2–3 tbs Grand Marnier, rum or almost
   any other liqueur

8 fl oz (225ml) whipping cream
a little cocoa and icing sugar or drinking
   chocolate

Tie a band of doubled greaseproof or Bakewell paper round a 1 pt (600ml) soufflé dish to come 2" (5cm) above the rim.

Put the eggs, yolks and sugar in a bowl, placed over a pan of hot water; the water should not touch the bowl and the water should not boil. Whisk the mixture over heat until thick, pale and forming 'the ribbon' when dropping off the whisk. Remove from the heat and continue whisking (less vigorously) until cold, standing the bowl in iced water to speed this up. Whip the cream until stiff, whisking in the Grand Marnier, then fold the two mixtures together gently. Turn into prepared soufflé dish and freeze for a minimum of about 8 hours.

To Serve. Serve frozen. It may need mellowing in the fridge for a while before serving. Remove the greaseproof paper carefully and sprinkle the top with a little cocoa and icing sugar mixed, or drinking chocolate, to make it look like a hot browned soufflé.

** Brandied Pears

This is a wonderful preserve. The sugar and brandy keep the pears indefinitely, and you can just dig into the jar whenever you want them. The pears shrink a lot in size, and of course the syrup is very sweet, so you only want a little in a glass, served with cream. The recipe is very old and comes from a friend in Northumberland. Make it when pears are plentiful in late autumn. Conference are good, and are not so prone to discolour as some others.

Ingredients

20 firm pears (preferably Conference)
sugar
rind of 1 lemon

3 cloves
½ stick cinnamon
¼ pt (150ml) brandy

Peel, core and quarter the pears, then weigh them and take ¾ lb (350g) sugar for each 1 lb (450g) pears. Place the pears, sugar, strips of lemon rind, cloves and cinnamon in a pan or large casserole and cook, covered, stirring from time to time, in a very slow oven (250°F/130°C/Gas 1) until the pears go pinkish-red and soft but do not break up, probably for 6 hours or more. Add the brandy and keep the pears in a jar for up to a year or more, removing what you need. Serve with cream.

F ✻✻   # Tarte au Citron

This sharp lemon curd flavoured tart in its crisp pastry is a great favourite all the year, but perhaps most useful in early spring when fruit or other fillings can be expensive. This is excellent from the freezer, either cold or slightly re-warmed, and is nice for large parties.

Ingredients
4–6 people

Pastry
6 oz (175g) plain flour
3 tbs icing sugar
4 oz (100g) firm butter
1 egg yolk
1–2 tbs iced water
pinch salt

Filling
grated rind and juice 1 lemon
2½ oz (60g) butter
2 eggs
3 oz (75g) castor sugar

Pastry. Sift the flour, salt and icing sugar into a bowl or the food processor. Add the firm butter, cut up into hazelnut-sized pieces, and rub in or process to the breadcrumb stage. Bind with the yolk and a very little cold water. Form into a flat disc and rest for ½–2 hours in the fridge in a plastic bag.

Roll the pastry to fit a 9" (24cm) removable base flan-tin. Prick the pastry, line with tinfoil and baking beans and bake in a hot oven (400°F/200°C/Gas 6) for 8–10 minutes until the pastry is set. Remove the tinfoil and return to a moderately hot oven (375°F/190°C/Gas 5) until golden brown and almost cooked.

Filling. Gently melt the butter. Lightly whisk the eggs. Whisk in the sugar and then the melted butter and grated lemon rind and juice. Pour into the pastry case and continue to bake in a slow oven (300°F/150°C/Gas 2) for 20–25 minutes until the filling has set. Serve hot, warm or cold.

$\mathcal{F}$ ** Blackcurrant Mousse

A fresh fruity mousse is always popular. This one can be made with fresh blackcurrants, in which case include a few of their leaves for flavour while they cook, or from frozen fruit at any time of year, in which case a stick of cinnamon can be cooked with them. The finished mousse freezes well.

Ingredients
4–6 people

12 oz (350g) blackcurrants
6 oz (175g) sugar
a few blackcurrant leaves (optional) or 1
    stick cinnamon
2 tbs *liqueur de cassis* (optional)
2½ teasp gelatine
2 tbs cold water
8 fl oz (225ml) whipping cream
3 egg whites
whipped cream and frosted
    blackcurrants to decorate (optional)

Place the blackcurrants, sugar, leaves or cinnamon stick in a saucepan with a little water. Cook until tender, then remove leaves or cinnamon and purée and sieve the blackcurrants. Stir in *cassis* if used. Sprinkle the gelatine on to the cold water in a small bowl and soak for several minutes; then stand the bowl in a pan of hot water until the gelatine has completely melted. Add to the blackcurrants and chill until completely cold but not yet setting. Whip the cream until it just holds its shape and fold in, followed by the egg whites whipped until they just hold a peak. Turn into a 1½ pt (900ml) soufflé dish and chill or freeze. Decorate with whipped cream and frosted blackcurrants, if you wish.

Frosted Blackcurrants. Lightly whip a white of egg until mousse-like and dip small bunches into it, coating evenly. Then dip into castor sugar till coated all over, shake off excess and leave to dry on a rack.

$\mathcal{PF}$ ** Winter Fruit Salad

Sun-dried mixed fruit is steeped in china tea and flavoured with lemon and cinnamon. It's a nice winter dish, and it goes well with old fashioned Snow Cream with Rosemary (*see page 95*).

Ingredients
4–6 people

1 lb (450g) mixed dried fruit (peaches,
  apricots, pears, prunes, raisins and
  apples)
1½ pts (900ml) china tea or water (2 teasp
  tea leaves)
1 lemon
6 oz (175g) sugar or to taste
2″ (5cm) stick cinnamon

Soak the dried fruit for at least 12 hours in the cold tea or water. Take julienne strips from the lemon, blanch in boiling water for 5 minutes or until tender, then drain and refresh under the cold tap.

Drain the fruit, measure the liquid, and make up to 1½ pts (900ml) again with water. Place in a pan with sugar, cinnamon stick and lemon julienne and heat gently until the sugar has dissolved. Add the fruit to the syrup and simmer gently until tender. Remove the fruit and boil down the syrup for about 5–10 minutes until heavier. Add the lemon juice, pour over the fruit and chill before serving.

This will keep for a week in the fridge and is lovely for breakfast with muesli or yoghurt.

P *   **Snow Cream with Rosemary**

This lightly whipped and flavoured cream is almost a syllabub and should be made 12 hrs ahead. It can be served with Winter Fruit Salad or on its own in small glasses.

Ingredients
4–6 people

8 fl oz (225ml) whipping cream
⅛ teasp fresh rosemary approx
1 lemon
2 tbs sherry
2 egg whites
2–3 tbs castor sugar

Combine the cream with the very finely chopped rosemary, the grated rind and juice of the lemon and the sherry, and whisk until stiff. Whip the whites of egg until just holding a peak, then whisk in the sugar until stiff. Fold the whites into the cream and turn into a bowl or little glasses. Serve chilled.

℉ ✳✳   Gooseberry Double Crust Pie

By Whitsun the gooseberry bushes should be well hung with small green fruit. Cull them carefully to thin the crop; they will still be very hard and green, but will make a good filling for this double crust pie which uses a short, crisp pastry. The filling may be a little runny when hot but should be just right when cold, which I'm told is the traditional way to serve a Whitsun gooseberry pie, with lashings of thick cream, of course!

Ingredients	Pastry
4–6 people	8 oz (225g) plain flour
	½ teasp baking powder
Filling	2½ oz (65g) butter
1 lb (450g) green gooseberries	1½ oz (35g) lard
4 oz (100g) Demerara sugar or to taste	1½ oz (35g) castor sugar
1 teasp cornflour	3–4 tbs cream or milk
1 tbs cold water	good pinch salt

Filling. Top and tail the gooseberries. Mix the sugar and cornflour and put with the water and gooseberries, in a saucepan. Cover and simmer gently until soft and pulped. If it seems very runny, as it can be in a rainy year, add a little more cornflour mixed with a teaspoon of water. Leave to cool before using in the pie. You can add a few chopped leaves of sweet cicily, angelica or scented rose geranium, or later in the year cook a head of elderflower with the gooseberries, but for this first pie of the year I prefer pure gooseberry.

Pastry. Sift the flour, baking powder and salt into a bowl or the food processor. Rub or process in the butter and lard, add the sugar and bind with the cream or milk. Form into two flat discs of equal size and chill for ½ hour or longer in a plastic bag in the fridge, though you can use this pastry immediately.

   Grease a 9″–10″ (24–28cm) pie plate and roll one disc to fit. Fill with the cold filling (if the filling still seems rather runny, rub ½–1 teasp of cornflour into the pastry base; it thickens the filling and keeps the pastry from going soggy). Top with the second round, pinch the edges together, cut off excess pastry round the edge and decorate the pie, cutting a slit in the top to allow steam to escape. Cook in a hot oven (400°F/200°C/Gas 6) for about 10–15 minutes until brown, then lower the temperature to moderately hot (375°F/190°C/Gas 5) and continue to cook for a further 20–30 minutes until the pastry is crisp and brown right through. Serve hot, warm or cold.